This book belongs to

_____

In memory of

_____

who was my

_____

I Will
Remember
You

My Catholic Guide
Through Grief

By Kimberly B. Schuler

Illustrated by
Mary Joseph
Peterson, FSP

Pauline
BOOKS & MEDIA
Boston

Nihil Obstat:
    Rev. J. Brian Bransfield, STD
Imprimatur:
    ✠ Justin Cardinal Rigali
    Archbishop of Philadelphia
    March 15, 2010

The author gratefully acknowledges the invaluable contributions of Anne Joan Flanagan, FSP, whose inspired idea provided the foundation for this book, and of Maria Grace Dateno, FSP.

Book design by Mary Joseph Peterson, FSP

ISBN 0-8198-3704-0

Published by Pauline Books & Media, 50 Saint Pauls Avenue, Boston, MA 02130-3491

Printed in the U.S.A.
IWRY VSAUSAPEOILL2-11J10-10156 3704-0
www.pauline.org

Pauline Books & Media is the publishing house of the Daughters of St. Paul, an international congregation of women religious serving the Church with the communications media.

1 2 3 4 5 6 7 8 9   14 13 12 11

Contents

For My Parent or Guardian to Read

Dear Parent or Guardian,

Someone your child loves has died.

It may have been a parent, sibling, grandparent, aunt, uncle, cousin, unborn child, or friend. It's a very sad time for adults and children alike. Sometimes it's too easy to forget the impact that death and grief can have on a child. It can be an overwhelming, confusing, and scary time. Their world has drastically changed, and they are struggling to make sense of all that has happened. They are in need of adult guidance and support to navigate this path.

This book, intended for children of elementary school age, can assist your child through the grieving process while helping them to honor the memory of their loved one. In child-friendly terms, *I Will Remember You* addresses death, grief, and how God and our Catholic faith can help your child through this sad time. It includes activities to allow your child to better understand grief and to remember his or her loved one in their own special way. There's also a "Special Days" section at the end of the book that focuses on holidays and special occasions, including the six-month and one-year anniversaries.

Grief is a unique and deeply personal experience; it has no timeline. Each child will progress through this difficult experience in her or his own way and own time. Developmental ages and stages also play a role in each child's movement through grief. Sometimes children revisit a loss months or even years later

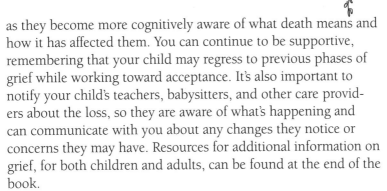

as they become more cognitively aware of what death means and how it has affected them. You can continue to be supportive, remembering that your child may regress to previous phases of grief while working toward acceptance. It's also important to notify your child's teachers, babysitters, and other care providers about the loss, so they are aware of what's happening and can communicate with you about any changes they notice or concerns they may have. Resources for additional information on grief, for both children and adults, can be found at the end of the book.

I recommend that you spend time with your child discussing the information and activities in this book. There may be times when he or she will have more questions or will need someone trusted to grieve with. Be open to conversations about death, loved ones, and faith. Children are very concrete in their understanding of the world around them. Death and heaven may be difficult and abstract concepts for a child. They may not grasp the permanence of death or the intangibility of heaven. Acknowledge your child's fears about death while encouraging a positive view of life, both current and eternal. And remember that you, too, are grieving. It's perfectly fine for your child to see you dealing with your own feelings of sadness. By seeing how you are coping with your grief (crying, praying, talking with others, getting counseling, etc.), your child may find new ways to express his or her feelings. It may also give him or her comfort to know that, even though you are all hurting, you'll work through this tough time together.

Through your love and support, their faith, and the love of God, your child will find peace again. God will be with your child, and you, always.

In Christ,
Kim Schuler

For Me to Read

Dear Reader,

Your parent (or another adult) has bought this book to help you during a very sad time. Someone you love has died. That person may have been a grandparent, an aunt, an uncle, or a cousin. It might have been a neighbor or a friend. It may even have been a sister, a brother, or one of your parents.

Lots of different things are happening around you. Many feelings are coming and going. It can be a very confusing time. But here's something to remember: What you're feeling is normal. It's called grief (pronounced GREEF). You're sad and hurting that someone you love is no longer here with you. It might be hard to believe right now, but in time you'll feel better. That doesn't mean you'll forget your loved one. It's just that as time passes, it won't hurt as much or make you feel as sad.

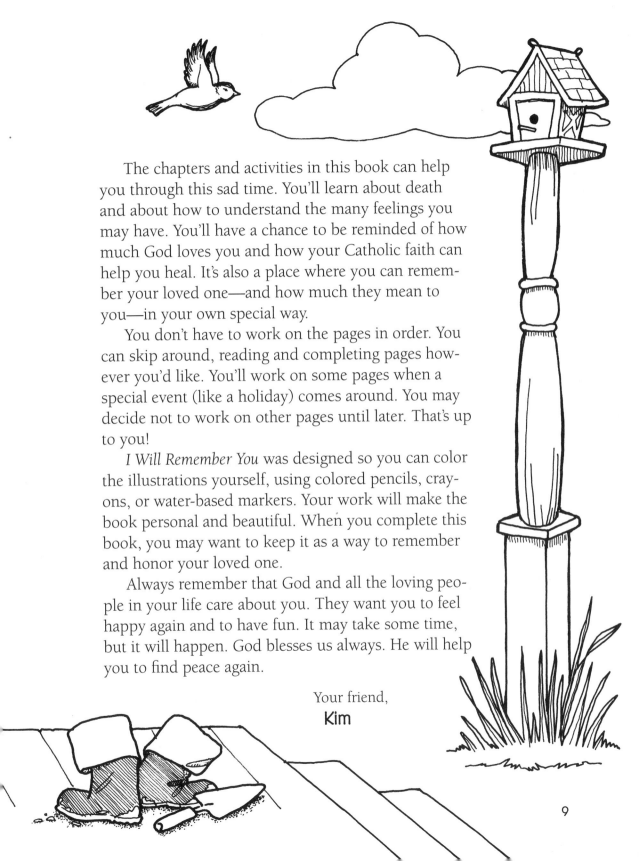

The chapters and activities in this book can help you through this sad time. You'll learn about death and about how to understand the many feelings you may have. You'll have a chance to be reminded of how much God loves you and how your Catholic faith can help you heal. It's also a place where you can remember your loved one—and how much they mean to you—in your own special way.

You don't have to work on the pages in order. You can skip around, reading and completing pages however you'd like. You'll work on some pages when a special event (like a holiday) comes around. You may decide not to work on other pages until later. That's up to you!

I Will Remember You was designed so you can color the illustrations yourself, using colored pencils, crayons, or water-based markers. Your work will make the book personal and beautiful. When you complete this book, you may want to keep it as a way to remember and honor your loved one.

Always remember that God and all the loving people in your life care about you. They want you to feel happy again and to have fun. It may take some time, but it will happen. God blesses us always. He will help you to find peace again.

Your friend,
Kim

About Me

My name is: _____

I am _____ years old.

Some of the people in my family are:

_____

_____

_____

Some of my friends are:

_____

_____

_____

A good place where I can be noisy is:

_____

A good place for me to have quiet time alone is:

_____

This is an outdoor game or activity I like:

_____

This is something I like to do indoors:

_____

A game or activity I like to do alone is:

_____

And here's something I like
to do with others:

_____

_____

11

This is something that makes me angry:

_____

Some safe things to do if I feel angry or frustrated
are: _____

_____

Something I worry about is: _____

Here's one thing that's safe for me to squeeze really
hard if I feel like it: _____

A helping grown-up I can talk to about how things
are going is: _____

Here are some things that make me happy:

_____

The Bible Tells Us . . .

Lord, you take
care of everyone
who loves you.

— Cf. Psalm 145:20

A Message for You

You're very
special to Jesus.
Remember that
he's always
with you!

Me and My Loved One

This book is about my _____, whose

name is _____.

Draw yourself
and your loved one
together in this
frame.

Tell about your
drawing. What
are you and your
loved one doing in
your picture?

_____

_____

_____

_____

_____

Favorites

✳ On one side, fill in your favorite things. On the other side, fill in your loved one's name and write his or her favorites. You may not be sure what their favorites were, but you can imagine what they might have been, or have a family member help you.

My Favorite Things

Color: _____

Animal: _____

Food: _____

Dessert: _____

Sport: _____

Sports team: _____

Song: _____

Book: _____

Game or toy: _____

Movie: _____

Holiday: _____

Place: _____

The Bible Tells Us . . .

"Even the hairs of your head are counted. So don't be afraid!"
— Luke 12:7

A Message for You

Jesus knows you and loves you.

_____'s Favorite Things

Color: _____

Animal: _____

Food: _____

Dessert: _____

Sport _____

Sports team: _____

Song: _____

Book: _____

Game or toy: _____

Movie: _____

Holiday: _____

Place: _____

My Memory Box

A memory box can be a place for you to keep special items that remind you of your loved one. Find a box with a lid, maybe a large shoe box. Cut out pictures and words from magazines that you like, or that remind you of your loved one, and glue them all over the box. Or cover the box and the lid with wrapping or construction paper, decorating it with markers. On the lid, glue a picture of the person you are honoring. While the glue dries, begin to gather the things you want to keep in this box.

✻✻ Here are some ideas for items you could put in your memory box:

✻ A memorial card or Mass booklet from the funeral

✻ Photographs of your loved one

✻ Recordings or audio files on CD of his or her voice

✻ A rosary, crucifix, or medal that belonged to your special person, or your own rosary, crucifix, or medal

✻ Jewelry, tie, or another small item owned by your loved one

✻ A small piece of fabric cut from a piece of your loved one's clothing

✻ Letters or cards

✻ Prayer cards or holy pictures

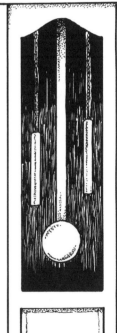

As you work through this book, you'll see suggestions for even more items you can add to the box. You may need a grown-up's help or permission to do some of the projects or to obtain some of the items you want to keep in the memory box.

What other things can you think of to put in your memory box?

_____

_____

 Where will you keep your memory box? Prepare a nice place for it, somewhere you can see and reach it easily.

I'm keeping my memory box

_____.

When your box is ready, place the items inside it. Then put your box in its own special place. Add things to the box as you are ready. Whenever you want, you can open it up to see and touch what you've put there. Whenever you're looking through the items in your memory box, you can think of your loved one. If you want to, you can say a prayer.

When you've finished with this book, you can keep it in your memory box, if it fits. Or you can store the memory box and the book together.

What Is Death?

It's such a sad time for you and your family. Someone you love has died.

But what does that mean? Well, when someone dies, it means that they are no longer here physically with us on earth.

So, where do they go? After he or she has died, God wants your loved one's soul to join him in heaven. Yet their body remains here on earth. He or she is no longer alive, because their soul is not united to their body anymore.

And what is a soul anyway? Well, a human person is a body and a soul united together. The soul is the spirit part of the person. The soul is the part of us that thinks and loves and knows what is right and wrong. We cannot see people's souls, but their bodies let us see the actions of their souls.

19

Through our bodies, we share our thoughts and feelings with others. For example, we can cry when we're sad, smile when we're happy, and talk with others about our thoughts and ideas. Our body also lets us hear and see the thoughts and feelings and ideas of others—like when we listen to what they say or watch what they do.

While we live here on earth, our soul and body are united. At death, the soul and body are separated. The body dies, but the soul lives forever. God wants the soul to enter heaven to live with him for all eternity.

Everyone's body will one day stop working. When it is time for our soul to meet God, it is called to join the souls of our loved ones who are already with God. In heaven, everyone is happy. There is no sadness or pain there. Everyone is honoring God and celebrating that they get to spend eternity with him.

This is why, even though we are sad when a loved one has died, we can look forward to seeing that person again. It will be a very, very long time from now, but God wants us all to be together in heaven with him one day. Heaven is so wonderful that we can't even imagine how much we will love being there!

Praying for Our Loved Ones
Who Have Died

You'll probably hear people saying that they are praying for your loved one. In this book, you'll also find suggestions to pray for your loved one.

Praying for someone who has died means asking God to take care of them and bring them to heaven to be happy with him. All good people go to heaven, but no one is good all the time. So, after a person dies, their soul may go *through* purgatory on the *way* to heaven. Going through purgatory is the way that a soul becomes ready to be with God forever. The souls in purgatory are called "holy souls," and they are happy because they know that soon they will be in heaven. We can pray for them, and they can pray for us.

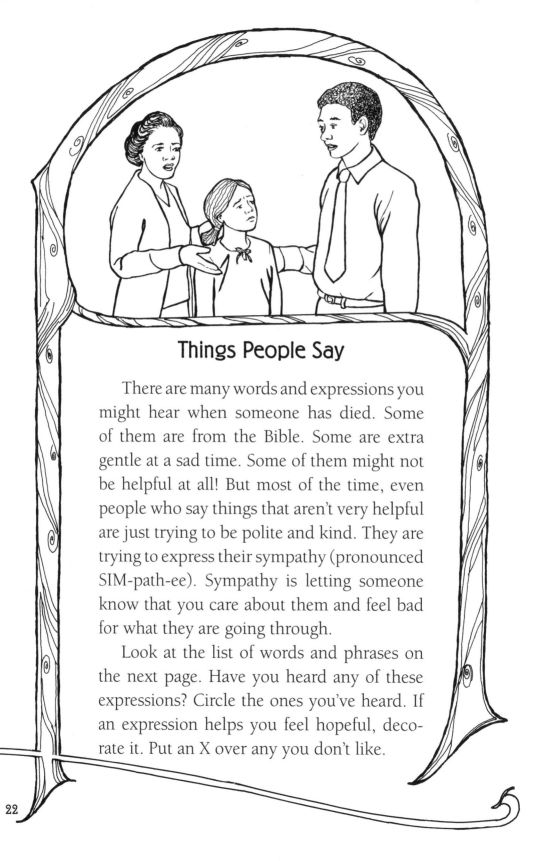

Things People Say

There are many words and expressions you might hear when someone has died. Some of them are from the Bible. Some are extra gentle at a sad time. Some of them might not be helpful at all! But most of the time, even people who say things that aren't very helpful are just trying to be polite and kind. They are trying to express their sympathy (pronounced SIM-path-ee). Sympathy is letting someone know that you care about them and feel bad for what they are going through.

Look at the list of words and phrases on the next page. Have you heard any of these expressions? Circle the ones you've heard. If an expression helps you feel hopeful, decorate it. Put an X over any you don't like.

Words and Phrases about Dying

Taken from us

Left us

Passed away

Gone

Departed

Gone to heaven

Words and Phrases about Heaven

A better place

A blessed relief

With the angels

God's will

At rest

God needed him/
her

Eternal rest
(eternal means
forever)

Repose
(this means at
peace or at rest)

Asleep in Christ

Words and Phrases That Mean
"People Who Have Died"

Faithful departed

Holy souls

Deceased (pronounced dee-SEEST)

Other Words and Phrases

※ Are there other words or phrases you've heard during this time that are new to you? Ask a caring grown-up to explain what they mean, and then write them on this page.

_____

_____

_____

The Bible Tells Us . . .

"I will be with you always, even until the end of the world."

— Matthew 28:20

A Message for You

Even if you feel confused by everything that is happening, remember that you can always talk to Jesus!

Words and Phrases that May Be Confusing

Grown-ups sometimes use the expressions "at rest," "asleep," or similar phrases when talking about someone who has died. That can be very confusing! When people die, they aren't resting or sleeping, and they're not going to wake up later. When adults use these phrases, what they really mean is that God wants the soul of the person who has died to now "rest" with him. They are happy and safe and not worried about problems anymore.

Sometimes people say that a person who died has become "an angel." Actually, people are people, even after they die. After they die, God wants their souls to go to heaven. But they don't turn into angels. Angels are made by God and are only ever angels. They were never people living on earth. But people in heaven are *like* angels because they are happy with God. They are watching over us, just as angels do. We can pray to our loved ones in heaven, just as we can pray to our guardian angels.

So Much Is Going On!

The Obituary

When a person dies, a special article is usually put in the newspaper, on the Internet, or both. It's called a death notice or an obituary (pronounced oh-BI-choo-er-ee). An obituary lets people know that someone has died. It's a way to honor the dead person and to show how he or she was important to family, friends, and community. It also provides important information to readers, including where and when the viewing and funeral Mass will be held.

Ask a grown-up if you can look at the newspaper to read your loved one's obituary. See who else died that day. Think about those people and their families, friends, and neighbors. Say a prayer for them.

🍂 Who was the oldest person who died that day?

Write that name here: _____,

age _____

🍂 Who was the youngest person?

Write that name here: _____,

age _____

For Your Memory Box

If you can get a copy of the obituary notice for your special person, add it to your memory box. Be sure to write on it the name of the newspaper and the date it appeared.

Be a Reporter!

❧ Write your own article, as if you were writing for the newspaper. Write the things you think are most important for people to know about your loved one who has died. Some of them might be the same as the newspaper obituary. Others might be different.

The Bible Tells Us . . .

"Everyone who has faith in me will live, even if they die. And everyone who lives because of faith in me will never really die."
— John 11:25

A Message for You

Everyone who loves God will live with him forever in heaven.

Obituaries are often listed online on the funeral home web site. Sometimes the online obituary will link to a memorial page where people can register to write messages of sympathy. Ask an adult for permission to log on to read these messages and to add your memories to the page.

_____, who was

_____ and

born on _____

died on _____, was my

_____.

One important fact about _____ is

_____

_____

_____

_____

Here's a special memory about this person:

_____

_____

_____

_____

What else do you want the world to know about
your loved one?

_____

_____

_____

_____

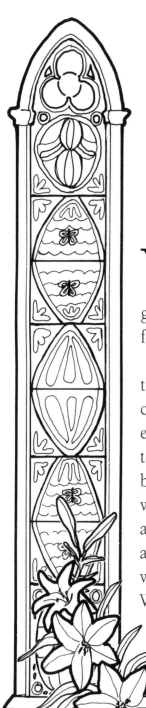

❧ The Funeral ❧

When a loved one dies, a funeral is planned. This is a time when family and friends gather to say a final goodbye to and pray together for their loved one.

The main parts of the funeral are the viewing, the funeral Mass, and the burial. In some families, children attend all three parts of the funeral. However, this may not be the case in other families. Talk to your parents or guardians to figure out what's best for you and your family. They may ask you what you'd like to do. It's okay if you want to go, and it's also okay if you don't. You can say good-bye and pray for your loved one in your own special way, even if you don't attend any part of the funeral. Whatever you and your family decide is all right.

The Wake or Viewing

The funeral usually starts with the viewing, sometimes called a wake. The viewing is a time when family and friends come to say good-bye to the loved one who has died. Viewings are usually held at funeral homes.

The rooms in a funeral home may look similar to living rooms. There are chairs and sofas. There may be pictures on the walls, small tables, and lamps around the room.

If you do go to the viewing, you'll probably see lots of flowers sent by friends and family. There may also be photos of your loved one around the room. Sometimes photos are placed on posters, or a video of photos may be playing on a television or computer in one of the rooms. There will probably be a guest book, too. Be sure to write your name in there, because the book will be another special item to help the family remember their loved one.

In the front of the main room you'll see the casket, sometimes called a coffin. This is the container for your loved one's body. It's usually made of shiny wood or metal. The inside of the casket may be lined with pretty, satiny cloth. The casket may be open or closed. If the casket lid is closed, you won't be able to see your loved one's body. But most of the time the casket is open, and that means the body of your loved one will be visible. Remember, the soul of your loved one is no longer in his or her body. The soul has gone to meet God.

People will spend time looking at the photos and talking to the loved one's family and friends. They may go up to the casket and say a quiet prayer for the loved one who has died. They may even share a silent message with the loved one, maybe about how much they will miss them or remembering the good times they had together. Sometimes people may place something special in the casket to be buried with the person who has died. It may be a prayer card, a note, a picture, or an item that was special to their loved one.

While praying and quietly sharing their messages at the casket, some people might stand; others may kneel. It's important to know that you don't have to go to the casket to say your prayer or to think about your message. You can sit in a chair or sofa and pray from there. Not everyone is comfortable with looking at a loved one's body after they have died. It's okay if you don't want to.

Near the beginning of a viewing, it's often very quiet. People are sad, and some may be crying. As time goes on, though, they often start to relax a bit. Sometimes they chat, and you may even hear laughter! That doesn't mean people aren't sad—they are. It just means they're feeling supported in their grief by the family and friends around them. And they may be sharing some happy memories together.

At some point during the viewing, a priest, deacon, or layperson may lead a Vigil Service. At a Vigil Service someone reads passages from the Bible and the people gathered at the viewing say prayers together. This is comforting for family and friends as they remember God's love for us, both in this life and in heaven.

There may also be a eulogy (pronounced YOO-leh-gee). This is a time when a friend or family member of the loved one may go up to the front of the room and share some of the things that made their loved one special. Sometimes the eulogy happens after the funeral Mass or at the cemetery instead of during the viewing.

🌿 Take a minute to think of a prayer or a message that you'd like to quietly share with your loved one who has died. Maybe you want to say what you'll miss about them. Maybe you just want to pray an Our Father or a Hail Mary. Write your message or prayer here.

_____

_____

_____

_____

_____

_____

The Bible Tells Us…

"I am the light for the world!"

— John 8:12

A Message for You

The light of God's love will always shine on us.

The Funeral Mass and Cemetery

For Catholics, the next event is the funeral Mass. Before the Mass begins, family and friends may gather together at the funeral home one last time. A priest may offer some prayers, and, if the casket was open, it's closed. Then it's time to drive to church for the funeral Mass.

The funeral Mass is like a regular Sunday Mass, but with extra prayers. The priest will also have special ways of blessing the body in the casket. The casket always remains closed during the funeral Mass. After the funeral Mass, family and friends travel to the cemetery (pronounced SEM-eh-ter-ee) where the body of the deceased will be buried. The body is usually in the casket. However, some people have decided that, when they die, they want their bodies to be cremated (pronounced CREE-may-ted).

Cremation is a special process that turns the body to ash. The ashes are then placed in a small, pretty container called an urn (pronounced ERN). If the body is going to be cremated, it usually happens after the funeral Mass. The burial services may then be on a different day rather than right after Mass.

The place in the cemetery where the casket or urn will be buried is called a grave. Sometimes the casket or urn will be placed in a small building called a mausoleum (pronounced moz-oh-LEE-um). A priest will often say prayers at the grave. Sometimes family and friends are given flowers and asked to place them on the grave. Other flower arrangements from the funeral home and the church may be brought there, too. After the prayers are finished, the family and friends of the loved one leave the cemetery. A headstone or marker is placed on the gravesite at a later time.

Here's a short prayer you will probably hear at the gravesite. The words *eternal* and *perpetual* both mean *forever*. Rest and light are ways we talk about how wonderful it is in heaven. The prayer asks God to bring our loved one to be happy with him in heaven.

Prayer for the Dead

Eternal rest grant to them, O Lord,
and let perpetual light shine upon them.
May _____,
and the souls of all the faithful departed,
through the mercy of God, rest in peace.
Amen.

✾ Draw or write about some of the things you saw at the viewing, the funeral Mass, or the cemetery.

For Your Memory Box

Create your own stained glass picture, like the beautiful stained glass windows in church.

Using tracing paper, trace the picture above. Color in the picture with crayons and then cut the picture out. Find a bottle of salad oil in your kitchen (ask an adult for permission). Put a small amount of oil on a paper towel or cotton ball and wipe both sides of your picture until it's covered with oil. Place the picture on paper towels or newspaper. When it's dry, bend a paper clip into a hook shape and hook it through the hole at the top. Hang the picture in a sunny window. After a while, you can move your stained glass picture into your memory box, but be sure to seal the picture in a plastic zipper bag first.

In Loving Memory

Sometimes families have memorial cards printed in honor of a person who has died. On the front of the card, there's a special picture, usually of Jesus, Mary, Joseph, or a special saint who's important to the family. The reverse side might show the person's name, the dates of their birth and death, and a prayer or special message.

The Bible Tells Us . . .

"You are now very sad. But later I will see you, and you will be so happy that no one will be able to change the way you feel."

— John 16:22

A Message for You

You will be happy again! Remember that you can always talk to Jesus.

For Your Memory Box

If you have a memorial card, be sure to add it to your memory box.

Here's a place for you to design and color your own special memorial card. You can draw and color a picture in the left-hand box and write your loved one's name and other information in the box on the right.

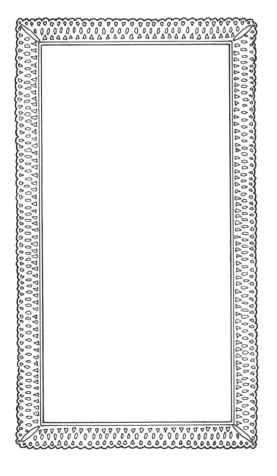

Grieving . . .

What Is Grief?

By now, you've probably heard people use the word "grief." Grief is another way of saying you're very sad that someone has died. Other words you may hear are "sorrow," "heartache," and "bereaved." These are all ways to say that you're sad and that you miss your loved one a lot.

Grieving and mourning (pronounced MORning) are words used to describe someone who is expressing their sorrow. When people are grieving, they may act in lots of different ways. For example, some people cry, others seem angry, and some may get very quiet or want to be alone. It's even okay to feel like crying one minute and then want to play a few minutes later.

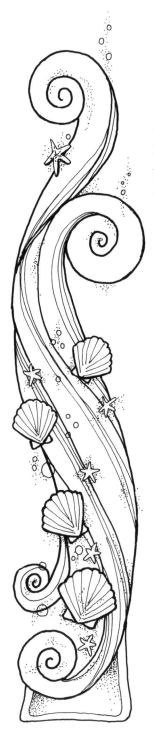

Things I've Noticed

What things have you noticed in the way people around you are mourning? Circle the things you've noticed others doing. Put a star next to the things you've done yourself as you grieve. Write or draw a picture for any words you don't find listed.

Crying	Daydreaming
Sniffling	Being cranky
Keeping busy	Acting distracted
Being quiet	Staying alone
Acting nervous	Pretend-smiling
Praying	Having a hard time sitting still

Even if you're really upset or angry, it's not okay to mourn by breaking, throwing, or hitting things. If you feel like showing your grief by doing something that might hurt you or someone else, you really need to talk to a trusted grown-up about what you're feeling.

While You're Grieving

Feelings of grief can come and go. Sometimes you may feel just as sad as you did the day your loved one died. Other times you may feel happy, as if everything is going fine. This is completely okay. It's also okay if you still feel sad weeks, months, or even a year later. Everybody's grief is different. Everyone's grief lasts for different lengths of time.

When you're grieving, your friends may not always know what to say or do. They're probably trying to be careful not to make you feel sadder.

The Bible Tells Us . . .

"God blesses those people who grieve. They will find comfort!"

— Matthew 5:4

A Message for You

Jesus loves you and will never forget about you.

But they may accidentally do or say something that hurts your feelings. They may even ask questions that upset you or make you think about your loved one when you don't want to!

Remember, this is a confusing time for your friends, too. They care about you and want to let you know they're thinking about you. They just aren't always sure how to do it. Let them know how you're feeling and that you'll spend time with them when you're ready.

Jesus and Mary Are Always with Us

At times, you may think no one else in the world knows how you're feeling. There are other people around you who are grieving, too, but sometimes you may still feel alone. Yet we're never really alone. We always have Jesus to turn to.

Here's a quote from the Bible, from Isaiah 49:16:

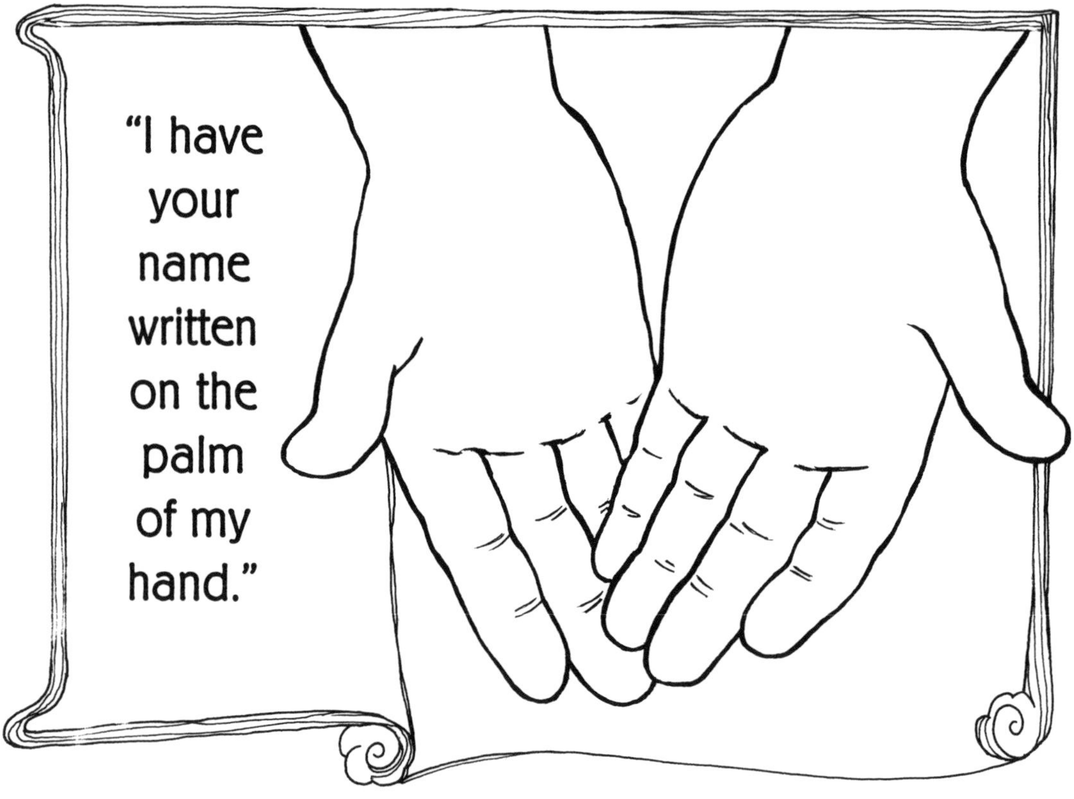
"I have your name written on the palm of my hand."

Write your name and your loved one's name on these hands.

Can you think of some other names that are written on God's hand? Write them, too!

Does that mean God wrote our names all over his hand with a pen? No, of course not! It's just a way of saying that God holds us close and cares for, looks after, and loves us forever. So right now, even while you're grieving, God is holding you close. He'll never let you go—no matter what! He also wants to hold your loved one close to him forever. God wants your special person to be with him.

We also have Mary, Jesus's mother, to turn to. She knows what it's like to live through the death of a loved one. Mary watched her son Jesus die on the cross. She understands our sadness and grief, because she's felt the same way.

When you're feeling sad or alone, you can say a prayer to Mary, our Blessed Mother. Mary has her own special prayer called the Hail Mary. You can say that prayer, make up your own, or even just talk to Mary about what you're feeling. No matter how we pray to Mary, she will listen.

Hail Mary

Hail Mary, full of grace,
the Lord is with you.
Blessed are you among women,
and blessed is the fruit of your womb, Jesus.
Holy Mary, Mother of God,
pray for us sinners
now and at the hour of our death.
        Amen.

My Prayer Shrine

If you like, you can set up a shrine to Mary in your house. (A shrine is a place to honor Our Lord, the Blessed Mother, or a saint.) If your family has a statue of Mary, ask permission to use it. If not, draw a picture of her (you can copy the picture in this book if you like). Tape or glue the picture to a piece of cardboard and decorate it. Put the statue or drawing on a table or dresser in your bedroom. Pick some flowers and arrange them in a vase beside the figure of Mary. If you like, you can write a prayer or message to her and place that on the shrine, too. You can also add something that reminds you of your loved one, like a photo, favorite flower, crucifix, or rosary. This shrine will help you to remember that Mary, our heavenly Mother, is always with you and always ready to help you when you're sad.

The Bible Tells Us...

"I will comfort them and turn their sorrow into happiness."

— Jeremiah 31:13

A Message for You

Jesus and Mary are always ready to help us.

51

In Denial

I Can't Believe It!

It can't be real!
"It's not true!"
"This can't be happening!"

Those are all things that might come to our minds when we're trying to understand that a loved one has died . . . and won't be coming back.

When we hear the news about the death of someone we love, it may be hard to believe. We want to think it's not true. Another word for this is denial (pronounced dee-NYE-al). Denial is having a hard time believing that something happened, even though it really did happen.

Sometimes when we're in denial about a loved one's death, we don't want to think or talk about them being gone. We might not want anyone else to talk about it, either! We really, really want to keep believing that everything is the same as before and that our loved one is still with us. If we refuse to believe what happened, then maybe we won't have to feel sad, or hurt, or angry, or any of our other difficult feelings. If we pretend that nothing has changed, then maybe we don't have to be upset or cry or worry about what happens next.

In time, the news of your loved one dying will seem more real and the denial will begin to go away. You'll begin to understand that it *is* true and that it's painful. It's sad and it hurts to lose a loved one. But refusing to believe it really won't change things.

❧ Where were you when you found out that your loved one had died?

_____

❧ Who told you the news?

_____

❧ What did they say to you?

_____

_____

_____

_____

❧ What did you think when you heard the news?

_____

_____

_____

✳ When people get news like this, some cry, hug, or say a prayer. Some talk about what happened. What did you say or do?

_____

_____

_____

_____

✳ Sometimes, when someone has died, family members gather together at a home, at church, or even at a hospital, if that's where the person has died. They might talk or cry together. Did you and your family do any of these things? What did you do?

_____

_____

_____

_____

_____

Jesus, Our Good Shepherd

In the Bible, Jesus tells us that he is the Good Shepherd and we are his sheep. He tells us that he will always care for us and love us, in this life and after we die. When we think of Jesus as our Good Shepherd, it reminds us that the person who died is safe with Jesus, just as a good shepherd protects a flock of sheep. It's true! And when we spend time with Jesus—thinking about him, talking to him, praying to him, or receiving him in Holy Communion—we are also close to those who have died.

Put a check in the box beside each place you've seen the image of the Good Shepherd:

- ❑ Stained glass windows
- ❑ Holy cards
- ❑ Paintings
- ❑ Statues
- ❑ Carvings
- ❑ Books

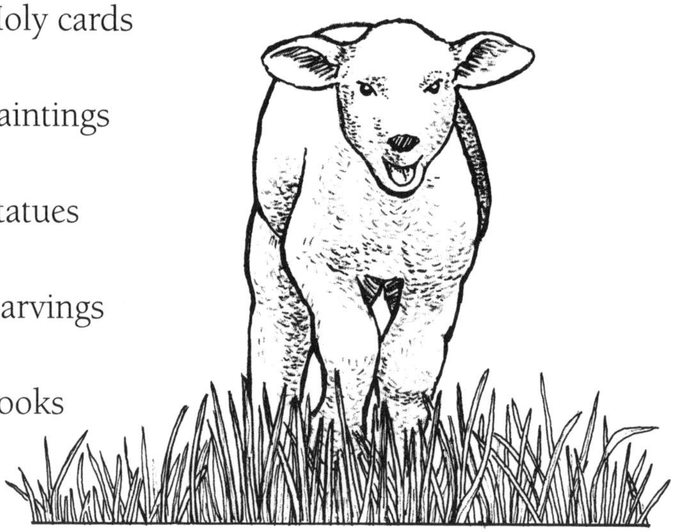

The Bible Tells Us . . .

"My sheep hear my voice, and I know them. They follow me, and I give them eternal life, so that they will never be lost."

— John 10:27–28

Connect the dots to finish the picture of the Good Shepherd.

Psalm 23

"The Lord is my shepherd; I shall not be in want."

This is the first line of a well-known passage from the Bible. It's a special kind of poem called a Psalm (pronounced SALM). This Psalm tells us that God will always be with us, no matter what.

Psalm 23

The LORD is my shepherd, I shall not be in want.

This means that God is our protector. He watches over us and takes care of us.

He makes me lie down in green pastures,
he leads me beside quiet waters,
he restores my soul.

God will help us rest and to find peace in our lives, and he'll give us support.

He guides me in paths of righteousness
for his name's sake.

God gives us strength during difficult times. He guides us to do the right thing in his name.

Even though I walk
through the valley of the shadow of death,
I will fear no evil,
for you are with me;

your rod and your staff,
they comfort me.

*When things are really bad or sad,
we don't have to be afraid. We're not
alone. God is always with us. He helps,
leads, and comforts us in tough times.*

You prepare a table before me
in the presence of my enemies. You anoint my
head with oil; my cup overflows.

*God will be with us even when it feels as if no one's
around to help. He's there for us in good and bad times.*

Surely goodness and love will follow me
all the days of my life,
and I will dwell in the house of the LORD
forever.

*God will love and care for us not just while we are on
earth, but also in heaven. God wants us to be with him
forever in heaven.*

We can turn to God whenever we need him. And it doesn't just have to be for really big or important things. God is always there to listen to our prayers— prayers for support and prayers of thanks.

✸ Can you think of some tough times when you might need to talk to God about a problem you are having? Take a look at the list below and circle the times when you could pray to God for extra support and strength. Draw or write about other times that you don't see listed here.

Fighting with your brothers or sisters

Accidents that hurt you or someone else

Arguing with your parents

Death of a loved one

Having problems in school

Moving to a new house

Going to a new school

Death of a pet

A Message for You

Jesus will always
keep us safe
in his love.

Acts of Kindness

Even though you may be feeling sad a lot, one way to add joy back into your life is to bring happiness to someone else.

Using colored paper, cut out some squares (or other shapes), about 3 x 3 inches. Think about kind acts you could do that might brighten the day of someone you know. They can be very simple acts such as: "I'll set the table." "I'll offer to take out the trash." "In the school lunchroom, I'll sit with someone who looks lonely." "I'll say something nice to my brother or sister," or "I'll read a story to a younger child." Write down your kind acts, one on each square. Fold the papers and put them into an envelope, bowl, or bag.

Then, each day—or whenever you feel like it—reach in and pull out one of the papers. That day, do the kind act that's written on that square. Some people may be really happy about the nice thing you've done. Some people may not even notice it much. But that doesn't matter, because doing something kind for others usually makes us feel good no matter how the other person reacts.

For Your Memory Box

Do the Acts of Kindness activity again, but this time, on the pieces of paper, write down some nice things you remember your loved one doing for you or others. Fold the papers and put them in your memory box.

Dealing with Anger

I'm So Angry!

Anger may seem like a strange feeling to have when someone dies. Why would anyone feel that way?

Well, there may be lots of reasons. You may feel angry because that person isn't with you anymore. You may feel angry because you didn't get to say "good-bye," "I love you," or other important things. You may feel angry because now that your loved one is gone, your life will change.

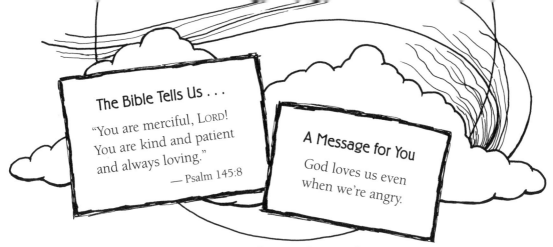

The Bible Tells Us . . .

"You are merciful, LORD!
You are kind and patient
and always loving."

— Psalm 145:8

A Message for You

God loves us even
when we're angry.

This angry feeling may be confusing, because you may even feel angry *with* someone, like the person who died, another family member, yourself, someone else, or even God. There could be many reasons why you're angry with those people, but no matter how angry you are, it isn't going to make your loved one come back.

God understands if we're feeling angry because we're upset and we miss someone we love. He loves and supports us in happy and sad times, now and forever, no matter what. If you're feeling angry at God or someone else, it may be very helpful to talk to a trusted adult.

It's important to remember that all the feelings we have are okay. It's okay to be angry, but we just have to be careful about how we act when we feel angry. It's NOT okay to hurt others, ourselves, or property with either our words or actions when we're angry. We have to handle angry feelings in ways that won't hurt anyone or anything.

Besides talking to an adult, another way to get out angry feelings safely is to write about them.

✺ Take a couple of minutes to write about your feelings. Why are you angry? Who are you angry with? You can have more than one answer for each question. Just go ahead and write it down.

_____

_____

_____

_____

_____

✺ There are lots of other ways to get the angry feelings out of our bodies and minds. Here are some ways to do that. Put a check in the box beside each one you think might be helpful for you.

❑ Talk to an adult

❑ Pray

❑ Play a sport

❑ Write a letter

❑ Draw

❑ Write in a journal

❑ Take a walk

❑ Play with a pet

❑ Take deep breaths

❑ Listen to music

❑ Dance

❑ Read a book

❑ Hang out with friends

❑ Say the Rosary or some other prayer that is special to you

❑ Spend time with your family

These are just some ideas to start with. Can you think of other things you could do to get out your angry feelings or to take your mind off feeling angry? Write some of your own ideas here.

_____

_____

_____

_____

_____

When you feel angry, try doing some of these things to help get your angry feelings out and to calm down. Afterward, come back and write about what your experience was like. What did you try? Did it help? How are you feeling now? What might you try next time?

_____

_____

_____

_____

_____

If Only . . .

Was It My Fault?

We say the words "if only" when we're wishing we could change things that have already happened. When someone has died, it's normal to think: "If only I could make it different." But you can't. Nothing you did made your loved one die. And nothing can be done that would bring your loved one back.

A Message for You

God will always forgive us and love us.

Sometimes you might have ideas like these: "If only I'd been better," "If only I didn't have those mean thoughts," "If only I was there when it happened," or similar things. The truth is this: none of your behaviors, words, or thoughts made your loved one die.

But you may feel bad about doing or saying something to your loved one that you wish you could take back. This feeling is called guilt (pronounced GILT). Guilt lets us know that we need to say we're sorry for what we did wrong. It lets us know we need to try our best not to do it again. Whatever you may feel guilty for, it's not your fault that your loved one has died.

Sometimes we haven't had a chance to say or do things that we wanted to say or do with the people who have died. There may be things you wish you had a chance to say to your loved one, like "I love you," "I'm sorry for . . .," or "I'll miss you." You may also wish you had been able to do certain things with them, like go on a special trip or vacation, watch a favorite movie, get a favorite treat or meal, make a special project with them, or play a game.

I Wish . . .

Write a note to your loved one telling them what you wish you could have said to them or done with them before they died. If there are things you wish you could change or say you're sorry for, you can write those too.

Dear _____,

_____

_____

_____

_____

_____

_____

Love,

_____

The Bible Tells Us . . .

" . . . I will have mercy and
love you forever.
I, your protector and LORD,
make this promise."

— Isaiah 54:8

Guilt and Relief

Another confusing feeling that sometimes makes us feel guilty is relief. We may feel relieved when something that's hard to deal with becomes less painful or worrisome. For example, if a loved one has been very sick or in pain, you may hear grown-ups say it was a "relief" or a "blessing" that the loved one died. That doesn't mean they wanted it to happen! They just didn't want their loved one to suffer any more pain or hurt.

After someone dies, you may also feel relief that your loved one is no longer sick or in pain. Things in your life may have been difficult while a loved one was ill or suffering. Maybe people were always too busy, or fighting, or crying a lot. Maybe you had to change things you did or places you went because of your loved one's pain or illness. Maybe you said, "If only . . . " and wished things were different and could be more normal again.

You may feel relief that things might go back to being more normal, or even easier, now that your loved one has gone to meet God. But that relief may also make you feel guilty. It's okay if you wished your life would go back to the way it was. Those hopes didn't make your loved one die sooner, and it doesn't mean you didn't care about them. It's okay to feel relief that your loved one's suffering is over, and that now things may get a little easier for everyone. Just know that it will take some time for things to go back to the way they were before. And sometimes things won't ever be exactly the same as they were.

The Bible Tells Us . . .

"Our LORD, we belong to you.
We tell you what worries us, and you won't let us fall."
— Psalm 55:22

A Message for You

God will help us through hard times, no matter what.

What's the Prayer?

A 1	J 10	S 19
B 2	K 11	T 20
C 3	L 12	U 21
D 4	M 13	V 22
E 5	N 14	W 23
F 6	O 15	X 24
G 7	P 16	Y 25
H 8	Q 17	Z 26
I 9	R 18	

___ ___ ___ ___ , ___ ___ ___ ___ ___ ___ ___ ___ ___
12 15 18 4   8   5 12 16 13 5   20 15

___ ___ ___ ___ ___ ___ ___ ___ ___ ___ ___
18 5 13 5 13 2 5 18 20 8 1 20

___ ___ ___ ___ ___ ___ ___ ___ ___
14 15 20 8 9 14 7   9 19

___ ___ ___ ___ ___ ___ ___ ___ ___ ___ ___ ___ ___
7 15 9 14 7   20 15   8 1 16 16 5 14

___ ___ ___ ___ ___ ___ ___ ___ ___ ___ ___ ___ ___
20 15 13 5   20 15 4 1 25   20 8 1 20

___ ___ ___ ___ ___ ___ ___ ___ ___ ___ ___ ___ ___ ___ ___
25 15 21   1 14 4 9   20 15 7 5 20 8 5 18

___ ___ ___ ___ , ___ ___ ___ ___ ___ ___ . ___ ___ ___ ___ .
3 1 14 20   8 1 14 5 12 5   1 13 5 14

Lord, help me to remember that nothing is going to happen to me today that you and I together can't handle. Amen.

I'm Still So Sad

Will I Ever Feel Happy Again?

When a loved one dies, it's normal to feel hurt and sad. And we may be sad for quite a while— weeks, months, even years. But then, as time goes on, we'll probably start to have times when we feel better and happier. We may start to have some fun with our family and friends again, even though we may still feel sad sometimes.

A Message for You

In time, you'll feel better. Jesus will help you find peace.

Some things that might help you feel better when you're very sad could be: playing with your favorite game or toy, inviting a best friend or special relative over, working at a hobby, writing in a journal, or drawing pictures of how you're feeling. If you have a pet, be sure to spend time together!

Sometimes when we're really sad, it can be helpful to remember things that used to make us happy. It may be remembering things we like to do with family, friends, alone, or even with the loved one who has died. It could be remembering things from home or school, indoors or outdoors. Sometimes just remembering names of people and places that make us happy can help.

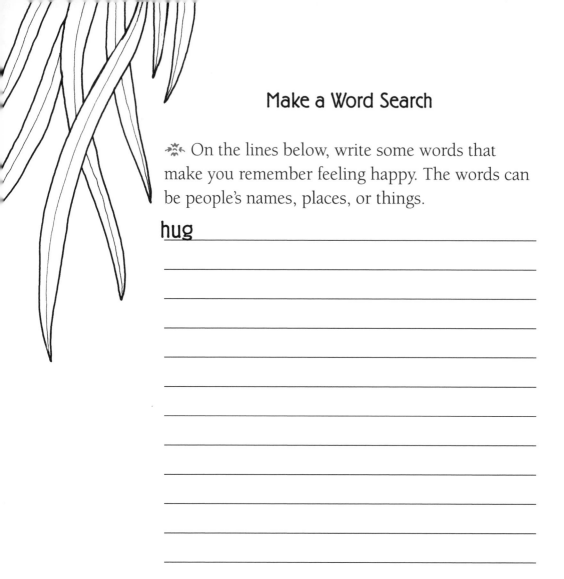

Make a Word Search

✹ On the lines below, write some words that make you remember feeling happy. The words can be people's names, places, or things.

hug _____

_____

_____

_____

_____

_____

_____

_____

_____

_____

✹ When you've filled in all the lines with your ideas, write the ideas in the puzzle by putting the letters in the boxes. You can go up, down, diagonally, and even backward! When you've filled in the puzzle with all the words you have, fill in the blank boxes with mixed-up letters until the whole puzzle is full.

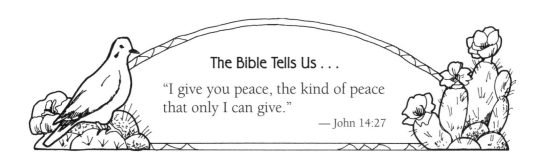

				H	U	G			

❊ Figure out what the date will be six months
from today. Write it here: _____

On that day, come back to this page and try to
solve your own puzzle. You can make copies of
this puzzle for a family member or friend to solve,
too.

When People Feel Really, Really Sad (for a Long Time)

For some people, after many months or more have passed, the feelings of sadness and hurt don't seem to get any better. In fact, they may even feel as if they're getting worse.

Feeling sad all the time, or almost all the time, for a long time is called depression (pronounced dee-PRESH-un). People who are depressed feel really, really sad most of the day, and even at night. They hardly ever feel happy anymore. They don't feel like having fun with their friends or their family. They may want to be alone a lot. They may cry. Some people may sleep more than usual, or they may find it hard to sleep at night. Sometimes people who are depressed may be in a bad mood and act cranky and mean. They may be afraid of things that never scared them before.

Depression is a serious condition. Most people who are grieving aren't depressed; they're just very sad. But if you believe you are feeling depressed, the most important thing is to talk to an adult you trust. It may be a family member, a teacher, a counselor, or your parish priest. Let that person know how you're feeling so they can help you. If the adult you talk to doesn't seem to understand, go to another trusted adult and explain your feelings to them.

No matter how you're feeling, you can pray and let God know about it. You could pray in your own words or say a prayer you've learned, like the Our Father, the prayer that Jesus himself gave to us.

Our Father

Our Father, who art in heaven,
hallowed be thy name.
Thy kingdom come,
Thy will be done on earth
as it is in heaven.
Give us this day
our daily bread,
and forgive us our trespasses,
as we forgive those
who trespass against us.
And lead us not into temptation,
but deliver us from evil. Amen.

✺ You can also write your own prayer here.

_____

_____

_____

_____

Going Forward

Healing and Acceptance

You may still have times when you're sad or hurting, but you also may be feeling a bit better now. Maybe you don't feel as terribly sad or angry as you once did. Maybe it's easier for someone to cheer you up. Maybe some things are starting to be fun again.

You're beginning to accept life after your loved one's death. Acceptance means that you believe what has happened and are adjusting to it; you're not in denial anymore. You still miss your loved one a lot, of course, but you're getting used to not having him or her here with you.

During this time of moving toward acceptance, you may even have mixed-up feelings again, like being happy or sad or angry at the same time. That's totally okay. God and your family understand that you're still hurting. Your pain is healing, and that takes time.

Sometimes you may feel guilty for being happy or for doing fun things again. You might even feel uncomfortable doing just ordinary things, like spending time with your family or friends. It's good to be happy again and to have fun doing ordinary things. Your loved one, who has gone to meet God, wants you to keep living the life that God gave you. Your special person wants you to be happy, even though you may feel it's hard to be happy sometimes. You're going on with your life, but you'll always have memories of your loved one in your heart.

All the mixed up feelings you may have had while you were grieving can come back. They may come back a little or a lot, for a long time or a short time. Some days, or even weeks, may go by when you're feeling fine, and other times you may feel sad or angry or hurt again. The thing is, there really is no way to know how long someone is going to take to grieve. Remember: this is all part of healing and acceptance.

No matter what, you're always going to miss your loved one. But over time, you'll probably be able to smile when you think about him or her.

Fly a Kite

On the kites above, write things you remember about your loved one. Even if you're still not ready to smile when you think of them, that's okay. Don't forget to decorate the kites, too!

Life Moves On

Here's a fact that may seem strange or uncomfortable: After someone important to us dies, we still have to live our own lives. At times it may seem hard and even unfair. But life for us on earth continues, even after a loved one has died. We have to wake up every morning and get ready for school, for church, for sports, and for other events. There are chores to be done and homework to finish, people to talk to and places to be. Life moves on.

The Bible Tells Us . . .

"For you shall go out in joy, and be led back in peace." — Isaiah 55:12

A Message for You

Always remember that God loves you!

What are some of the day-to-day things you often do? Circle them and write in others that you don't see listed.

Clean my room

Go to school

Set the table

Do my homework

Care for a pet

Take out the trash

Brush my teeth

Eat my meals

Read books

Talk to friends

Play

Take a bath or shower

Ride the school bus

Get dressed

Listen to music

Go to church

Spend time with my family

_____

_____

_____

_____

Moving back into your routine—the ordinary things you do every day—doesn't mean that you're forgetting about your loved one who has died. You just may start to notice that you don't feel sad as much anymore. It may start to feel more natural to do ordinary things. And that's good. And your loved one who has gone to meet God will be happy to know that you are doing these things.

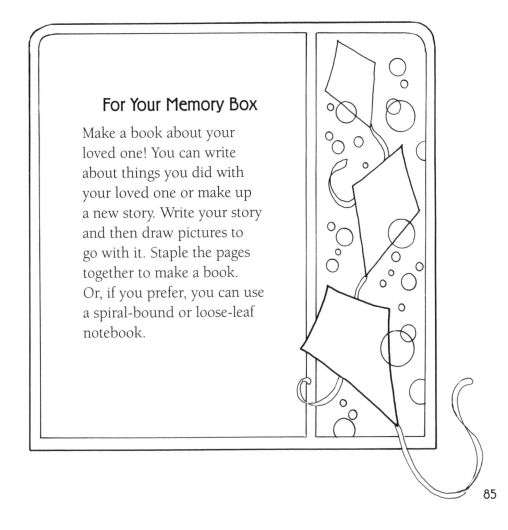

For Your Memory Box

Make a book about your loved one! You can write about things you did with your loved one or make up a new story. Write your story and then draw pictures to go with it. Staple the pages together to make a book. Or, if you prefer, you can use a spiral-bound or loose-leaf notebook.

It's Still a Wonderful World

This wonderful world that God created for us to enjoy may not seem so wonderful while you are grieving. Even though everyone feels sad sometimes, it's important to remember that there are still lots of special things in the world and in your life.

God made the earth—and everything around us—very special.

Let's think about the beautiful world God created. The picture on the next page has been started for you—it has land, water, and sky. But the world is full of many more things that God made for us, like the sun, the moon and stars, plants, animals, birds, fish, and, of course, people! Finish the picture by adding in the things that are missing. Be sure to include yourself and some of the people you love.

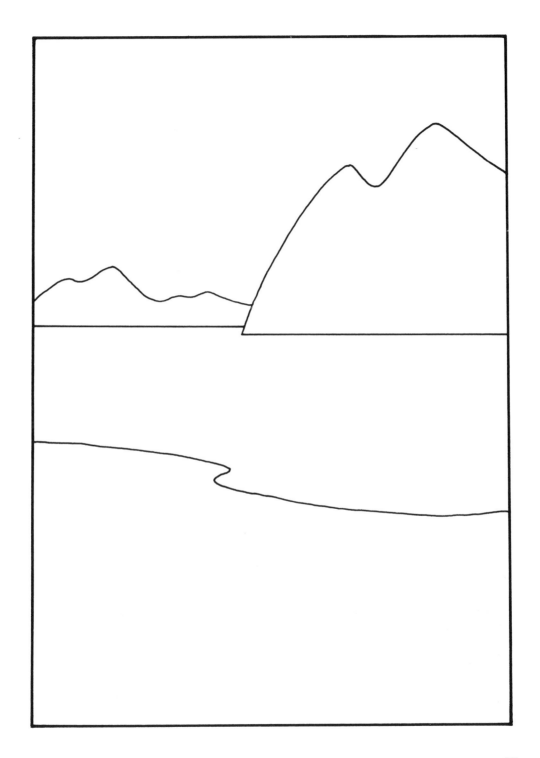

Now that you've finished drawing a scene of God's beautiful creation, take some time to think about the other wonderful things in the world that make you happy. God—and your loved one—want you to find joy in your life again.

A-Mazing!

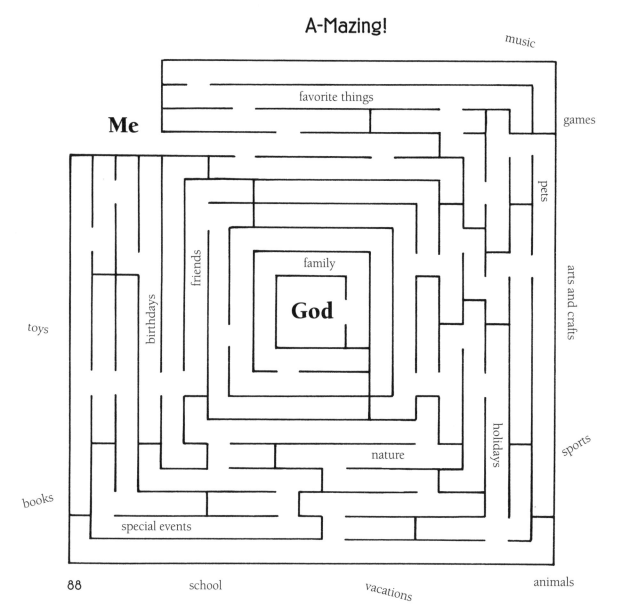

✳ What other things can you think of that make you happy? List them here.

_____

_____

_____

_____

_____

_____

The Bible Tells Us . . .

"You are the living LORD!
I will praise you! You are
a mighty rock. I will
honor you for
keeping me safe."

—2 Samuel 22:47

A Message for You

Even though the
seasons change,
God's love for us
never does.

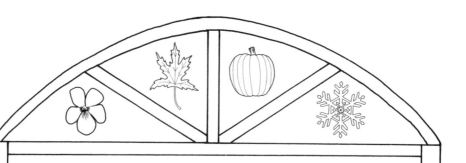

The Seasons of Life

We know there are four seasons in a year: spring, summer, fall, and winter. Each season in nature is important. Different and wonderful things happen during each season. They show us the beauty in the cycle of life and death.

In some parts of the United States and Canada, here's what may be happening during the four seasons:

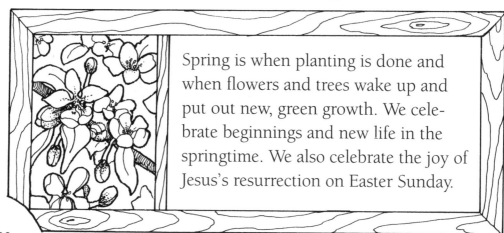

Spring is when planting is done and when flowers and trees wake up and put out new, green growth. We celebrate beginnings and new life in the springtime. We also celebrate the joy of Jesus's resurrection on Easter Sunday.

During the summer, crops grow tall and gardens bloom. The crops need the summer sun to become strong and healthy plants. In summer, animals enjoy plenty of food and the warm summer sun.

Fall is a time of harvest, the time when farmers' crops are gathered from the fields. In fall, we celebrate Thanksgiving, sharing our food and our blessings with family and friends. Animals begin to gather and store food for the coming winter months.

In winter, cold and snow blanket the fields, plants, and trees. Animals look for warm places to stay. It seems like a quiet time of the year in nature, because not many things are growing. It's a time of rest from a very busy year of planting, growing, and harvesting. It's also a time of waiting—waiting and preparing during Advent to celebrate Jesus's birth on Christmas Day.

The seasons may be very different in the part of the country where you live.

✳ Can you draw a picture of some things that are usually happening in nature during each of the seasons?

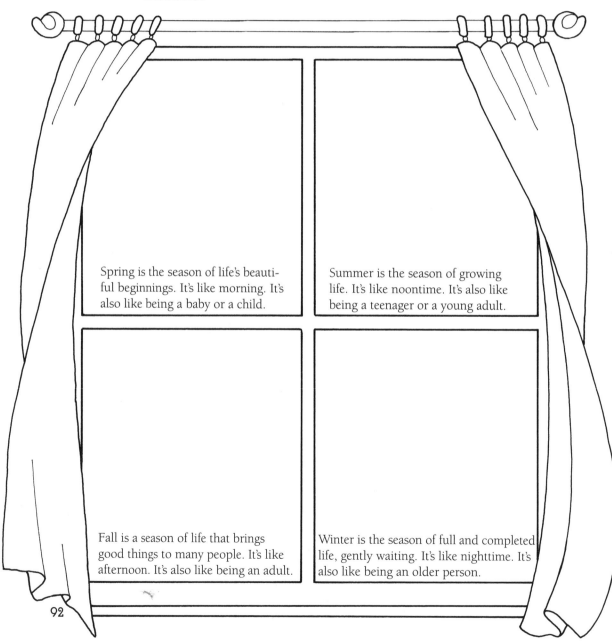

Spring is the season of life's beautiful beginnings. It's like morning. It's also like being a baby or a child.

Summer is the season of growing life. It's like noontime. It's also like being a teenager or a young adult.

Fall is a season of life that brings good things to many people. It's like afternoon. It's also like being an adult.

Winter is the season of full and completed life, gently waiting. It's like nighttime. It's also like being an older person.

Different and wonderful things happen to us in the seasons of our lives, too.

Think about your loved one.

What "season of life" was your loved one in when he or she died? For example, if your loved one was an older person (elderly), then the season of their life was winter.

_____

What are some of the wonderful things that happen during that season in nature?

_____
_____
_____
_____
_____

For Your Memory Box

Write a word poem about the season in which your loved one died. This is how to do it: On a piece of paper, write the letters of the season, one letter on each line. Think of things starting with that letter that remind you of that season. After each letter, write your idea that begins with that letter. The example below is a word poem that might apply to some parts of the United States and Canada, but your word poem should be about a season where *you* live.

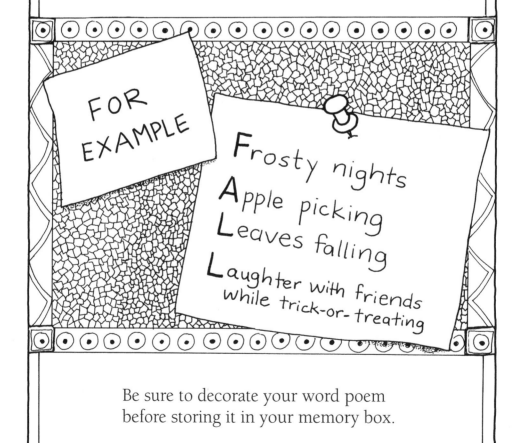

FOR EXAMPLE

Frosty nights
Apple picking
Leaves falling
Laughter with friends while trick-or-treating

Be sure to decorate your word poem before storing it in your memory box.

What's Next?

How You're Feeling Now

The pages that follow are special ways to help you remember your loved one during the year.

Lots of special days and holidays happen during the year. They usually make us feel very happy. But this year, and maybe for the next several years, you might find that these special days make you feel lots of different feelings—maybe all at the same time!

A Message for You

Remember that God, our loving Father,
sends us the gift of his love each day.

Special days may make you think of your loved one who has died, and how he or she is no longer here to celebrate with you. That may make you feel sad or even angry. You know your loved one has gone to meet God, but you wish he or she were here with you. For example, even if you feel happy because it's Christmas, at the same time you may feel sad that your special person isn't here. It's normal to have these kinds of mixed-up feelings. Lots of people do.

You might wonder why you're sad again. You—and maybe people who know you—might think you should be feeling better by now. But that's not how grief works. It doesn't just stop after a certain amount of time. It can come and go at all different times in our lives. At times, special days and holidays can make grief come back for a while, and mix in with our other feelings. Even when we think we're all finished grieving and back to living our regular, happy lives again, sometimes we can still feel sad or hurt or lonely.

The Bible Tells Us. . .

"I will bless you with a future filled with hope . . . ."
— Jeremiah 29:11

When grief comes back, it's important to remember the things you can do to help yourself feel better. It's important to remember that there are people you can talk to about it. Look back on the pages in this book to help you remember what to do when you are feeling sad, hurt, or angry.

Draw or write down some of the things you can do, or people you can talk to in the space below.

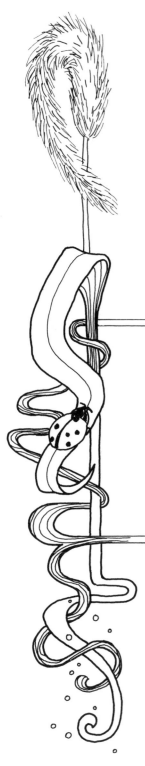

Before and After

Talking and thinking about your loved one may be easier now that some time has passed. But things like holidays and special events may remind you of how much you miss her or him. You might still feel sad sometimes, but maybe you now have some new memories, even happy ones, of things that have happened since your loved one died.

Special Times

❋ Draw a picture of a time in your life before your loved one died. Tell about the picture. What were you doing? Who else was with you?

_____

_____

_____

_____

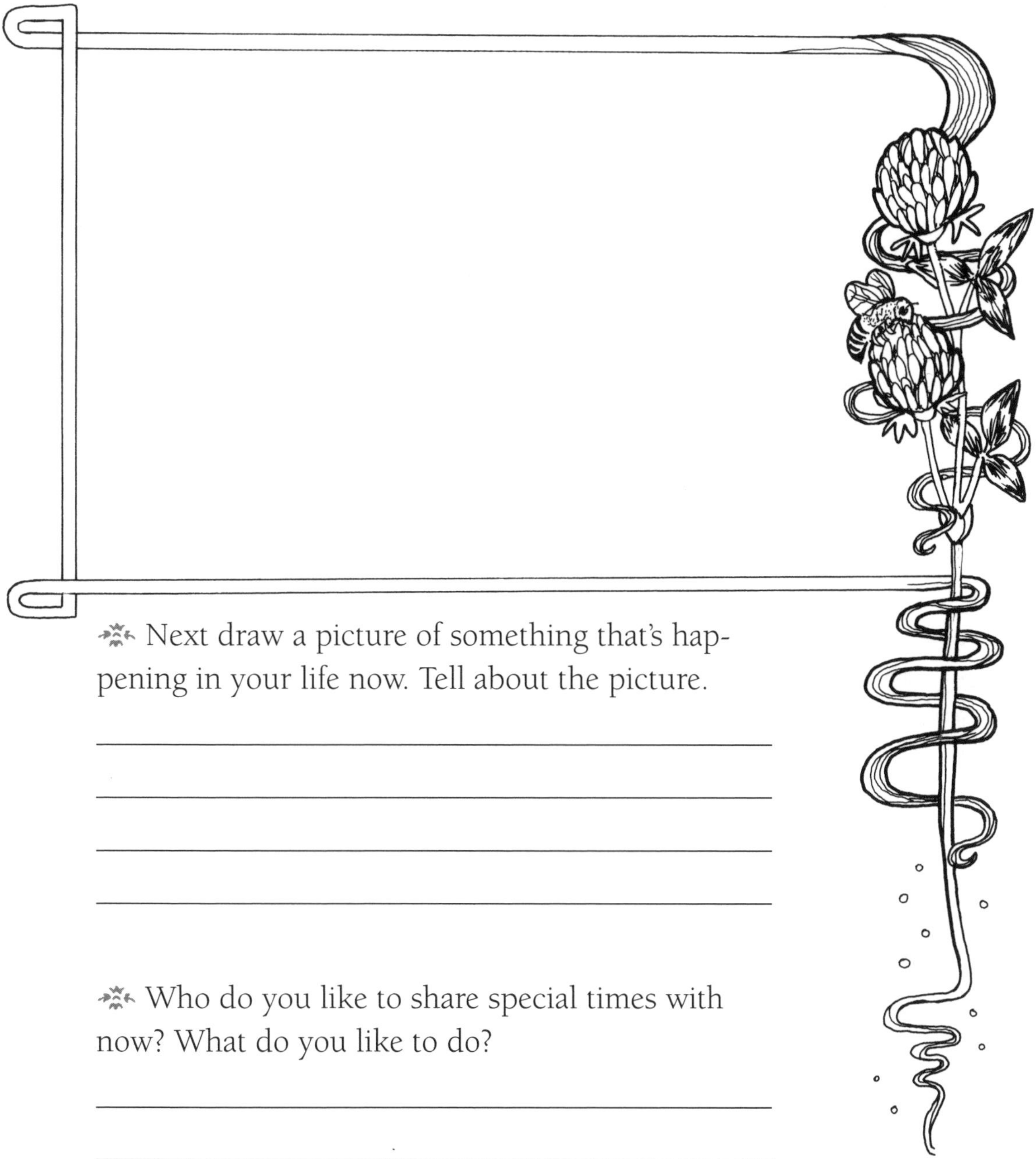

❧ Next draw a picture of something that's happening in your life now. Tell about the picture.

_____

_____

_____

_____

❧ Who do you like to share special times with now? What do you like to do?

_____

_____

_____

_____

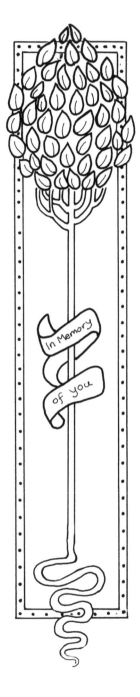

Honoring Your Loved One

After someone dies, there may be special things you can do to remember and honor them. Some people visit the cemetery to pray at their loved one's gravesite. While visiting, they might leave flowers, cards, candles, or other special objects. They may even leave something as simple as a small rock.

Some people may visit the cemetery very often or only once or twice a year, perhaps on holidays. But there are some people who may not visit the cemetery at all. It may make them too sad, or perhaps they have their own ways to honor the person they miss without going to the cemetery.

If you'd like to visit the cemetery to spend time at your loved one's grave, talk to an adult about taking you. But if you don't think you'd like to go there, that's perfectly fine, too. It's okay if you want to go, and it's okay if you don't want to. Either choice is normal. Either is fine.

At the Cemetery

If you want to, you can choose a rock to take to the cemetery. You can wash it, then paint it or write special words on it and leave it at the grave, if that's permitted, as a way to honor your loved one. (Be sure to use permanent markers or paint that won't wash off.) If you'd like to keep the rock at home to remember your loved one instead of leaving it at the cemetery, find a special place in your house where you can keep it, or keep it in your memory box. You can even decorate two rocks—one for your home and one for the cemetery.

Plant a Garden

Plant a garden at the cemetery, if it's permitted, or at your house to honor the person you miss. Have a grown-up help you choose one or more flowering plants and plant them. Remember to check the flowers every so often to be sure they're getting enough water.

If you can't plant flowers in the ground, you may decide to bring a plant in a pot and leave it at the gravesite or in a special place in your house for remembering. People sometimes even plant trees at cemeteries! You'd need an adult's permission and help for that.

Another way people may honor someone who has died is by spending more time praying in church. It makes them feel closer to God and to their loved one. Some families will ask for a memorial Mass to be celebrated on the anniversary of their loved one's death. Memorial Masses are regular Masses, but the prayers are said for the loved one who has died. You can talk to an adult about making arrangements for a memorial Mass.

For Your Memory Box

Create a photo album! Have an adult help you gather pictures of your loved one and place them in a photo album. You can use markers and stickers to decorate the pages and write about the pictures. When you're finished, you can keep the album in your memory box. If the album is too large, keep it near your memory box.

You might want to start a second photo album of new memories that are happening in your life now.

The Rosary

Saying special prayers or the Rosary are also ways people can honor and remember their loved ones all year. You can say the Rosary in remembrance of your special person whenever you want. Use the picture below to guide you.

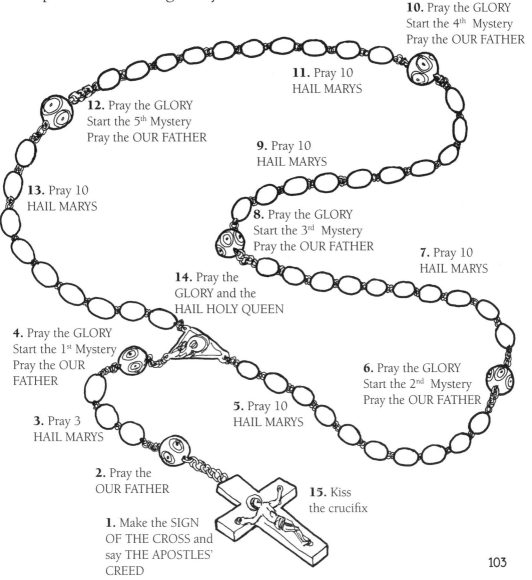

10. Pray the GLORY
Start the 4th Mystery
Pray the OUR FATHER

11. Pray 10
HAIL MARYS

12. Pray the GLORY
Start the 5th Mystery
Pray the OUR FATHER

9. Pray 10
HAIL MARYS

13. Pray 10
HAIL MARYS

8. Pray the GLORY
Start the 3rd Mystery
Pray the OUR FATHER

7. Pray 10
HAIL MARYS

14. Pray the
GLORY and the
HAIL HOLY QUEEN

4. Pray the GLORY
Start the 1st Mystery
Pray the OUR
FATHER

6. Pray the GLORY
Start the 2nd Mystery
Pray the OUR FATHER

3. Pray 3
HAIL MARYS

5. Pray 10
HAIL MARYS

2. Pray the
OUR FATHER

15. Kiss
the crucifix

1. Make the SIGN
OF THE CROSS and
say THE APOSTLES'
CREED

103

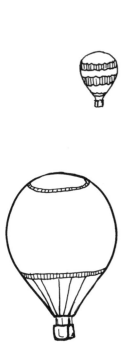

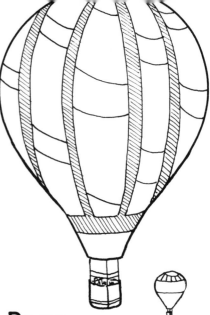

Special Days

My Six Month Page

The time to look at this page is about six months after your loved one died.

Today's date is _____.

The weather is _____.

Here's something interesting about today:

_____

Here's something I want to do (or already did)

today: _____.

I remembered my loved one, _____,

today by: _____

_____

_____

_____

Here's something my family is doing today:

_____

_____

_____

Use your imagination on this one: If I could go anywhere in the world today for one hour, it would be:

_____

_____

_____

Why did you pick that special place?

_____

_____

_____

Do you have a special six-month message for the person this book is dedicated to? Write your message here:

_____

_____

_____

Memories

✳ Using the boxes below, draw a comic strip featuring you and your loved one. You may want to illustrate one of your favorite memories, or you can imagine sharing a favorite activity with them today. Add speech bubbles in the boxes to show what each person is saying. Be sure to color in the comic strip, too!

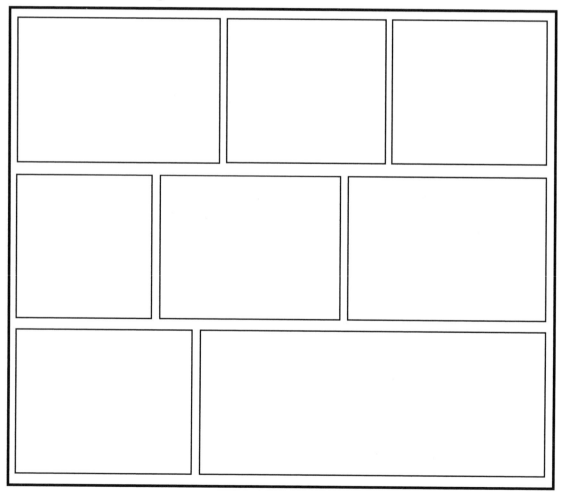

🌸 Go back to page 77 and try to solve the word search puzzle you created six months ago. If you want to save it to try again later, just make a copy of the page and solve the puzzle on the copy.

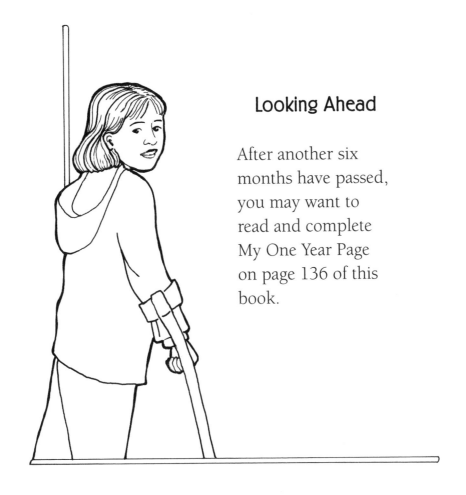

Looking Ahead

After another six months have passed, you may want to read and complete My One Year Page on page 136 of this book.

The Birthday
of Your Loved One

Birthdays are for celebrating. Just because a loved one is no longer with you doesn't mean you have to stop celebrating their birthday—but it might not be easy to do the first year, or even for a few years. When your loved one's birthday comes around, you'll be reminded that they're not with you anymore. This might make you very sad on a day that used to be filled with happiness.

In time it will be easier to remember your loved one's birthday, and it won't hurt as much to think about them and the happy memories that you shared.

Some families may decide to do something to honor a person who has died on their birthday. They may attend a memorial Mass offered for their loved one, visit the cemetery, or spend the day doing things enjoyed with that person. Are you or your family doing anything special to remember your loved one on their birthday? If you are, write or draw about it here:

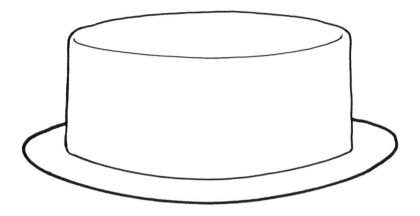

❉ Decorate the birthday cake with your loved one's favorite colors or colors he or she might have liked. Be sure to add candles!

❉ How did your loved one like to celebrate birthdays? Did they have a special place to go? A favorite food to eat? A favorite activity to do on their special day? Write about it here. You could also write about a favorite birthday memory you have of your loved one.

_____

_____

_____

_____

_____

✿ Using the space below, design a birthday card for you loved one. Write wishes, hopes, or prayers inside the card.

For Your Memory Box

Make another birthday card for your loved one that you can add to your memory box.

Your Birthday

Today's your birthday! It's usually a very happy day, but this year you may find it to be bittersweet—that is happy and sad at the same time. Of course you're happy that it's your birthday. But you're sad because your loved one isn't here to celebrate with you. It's okay to enjoy yourself on your special day. Your special person would want that. It's also okay if you aren't really in the mood for celebrating and just want to do something quiet with your family.

Dot-to-Dot

Connect the dots to read the message.

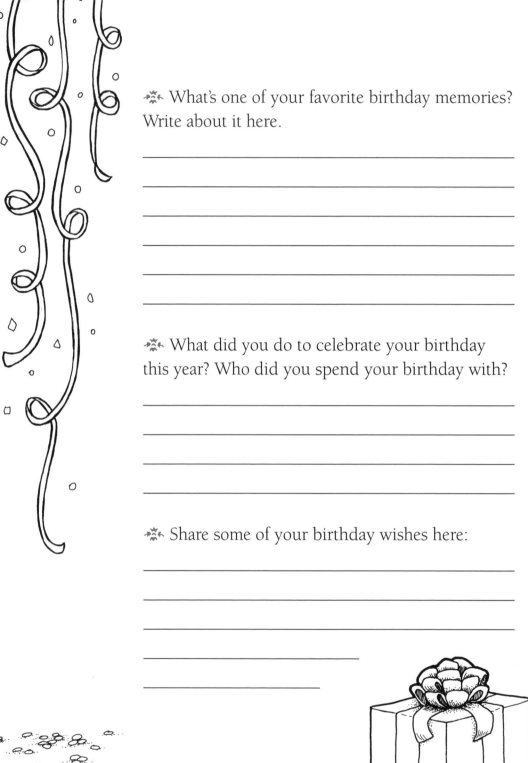

✵ What's one of your favorite birthday memories? Write about it here.

_____

_____

_____

_____

_____

_____

✵ What did you do to celebrate your birthday this year? Who did you spend your birthday with?

_____

_____

_____

_____

✵ Share some of your birthday wishes here:

_____

_____

_____

_____

_____

Decode It!

To find out the message below, write the first letter of each picture on the line. Don't forget to color the pictures when you've finished the puzzle.

___ ___ ___ ___ ___ ___ ___ ___ ___ ___ ___

1 2 3 4 5 6 7 8 9 10 11

___ ___ ___.

12 13 14

Peace be with you.

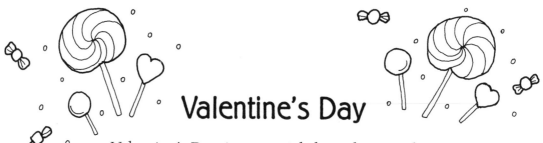

Valentine's Day

Valentine's Day is a special day when we let our loved ones know how much we care about them. On February 14, hearts and flowers are everywhere! They remind us about the great love Saint Valentine had for God and for people. Now Saint Valentine is in heaven, where everyone who loves God is happy forever.

Even though everyone in heaven may be happy forever, right now on earth you may not be very happy. You may be missing your loved one, and Valentine's Day may make you feel sad. But Valentine's Day is all about love—and the reason you're feeling sad is because you love and care about your loved one so much. What better time to remember all those you love, both living and deceased, than on Valentine's Day?

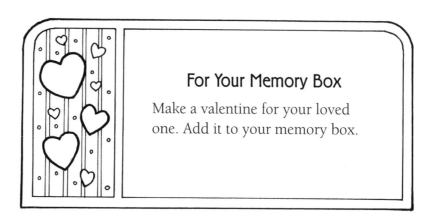

For Your Memory Box

Make a valentine for your loved one. Add it to your memory box.

Did you make valentines for any special people today? Who were they for?

_____

_____

_____

Did you get (or do you expect) any valentines today? Who were they from?

_____

_____

_____

Can you think of anyone who might need a special remembrance of love on this Valentine's Day? Gather some paper and crayons or markers to make a Valentine's Day card for them.

Color.

God is love, and those who live in love, live in God.

Easter

"God loved the people of this world so much that he gave his only Son, so that everyone who has faith in him will have eternal life and never really die" (John 3:16).

Jesus died and rose from the dead so that our sins would be forgiven and so that one day we can join God in heaven forever. We celebrate Jesus's glorious resurrection (pronounced rez-er-REK-shun), his rising from the dead, in a special way on Easter Sunday.

Easter is the biggest holiday of all for Catholics. It's so important that we don't just celebrate for one day. First we have forty days of Lent to prepare for Easter. The week right before Easter is called Holy Week. Then, we have the Easter Season that goes on for fifty days after Easter!

During Holy Week, we remember many things, some of them happy and some of them sad. There is happiness on Palm Sunday when Jesus enters Jerusalem and the people welcome him. There is joy and love when Jesus gives us the gift of the Eucharist on Holy Thursday. There is anger and sadness when Jesus is betrayed by Judas and then arrested. There is sorrow and grief on Good Friday when Jesus dies on the cross. And then there is great joy when Jesus rises from the tomb on Easter Sunday!

When we celebrate Jesus's resurrection, we may wish that our loved ones could also come back from the dead. Our loved ones won't rise from the dead to come back and live on earth. But God has made a special promise. We remember this promise every Sunday at Mass when we pray a long prayer called the Creed. The Creed says what we believe as Catholics. The last line of the Creed is: "We look for the resurrection of the dead, and the life of the world to come. Amen."

What does this mean? When all who love God are in heaven together, God has promised that he will give us a wonderful gift. Our bodies will rise from the dead like Jesus's, and our souls and bodies will be united again. Then we will be together and happy in heaven forever.

Symbols of Easter

Eggs are one symbol of Easter. They may be candy or chocolate, plastic or hard-boiled. You may even spend time with your family decorating eggs for Easter Sunday. But what do eggs have to do with Easter and Jesus rising from the dead?

Well, it's all about new beginnings. In springtime, new plants are growing, animals are having babies, and birds are hatching from their eggs. Lots of new things happen in nature during spring—everything is coming to life after the long winter. Eggs are a symbol of new life and growth. They're a symbol of Jesus's rising from the dead, his resurrection.

Eggs-actly

Gather your crayons or colored pencils and take some time to decorate the Easter eggs below.

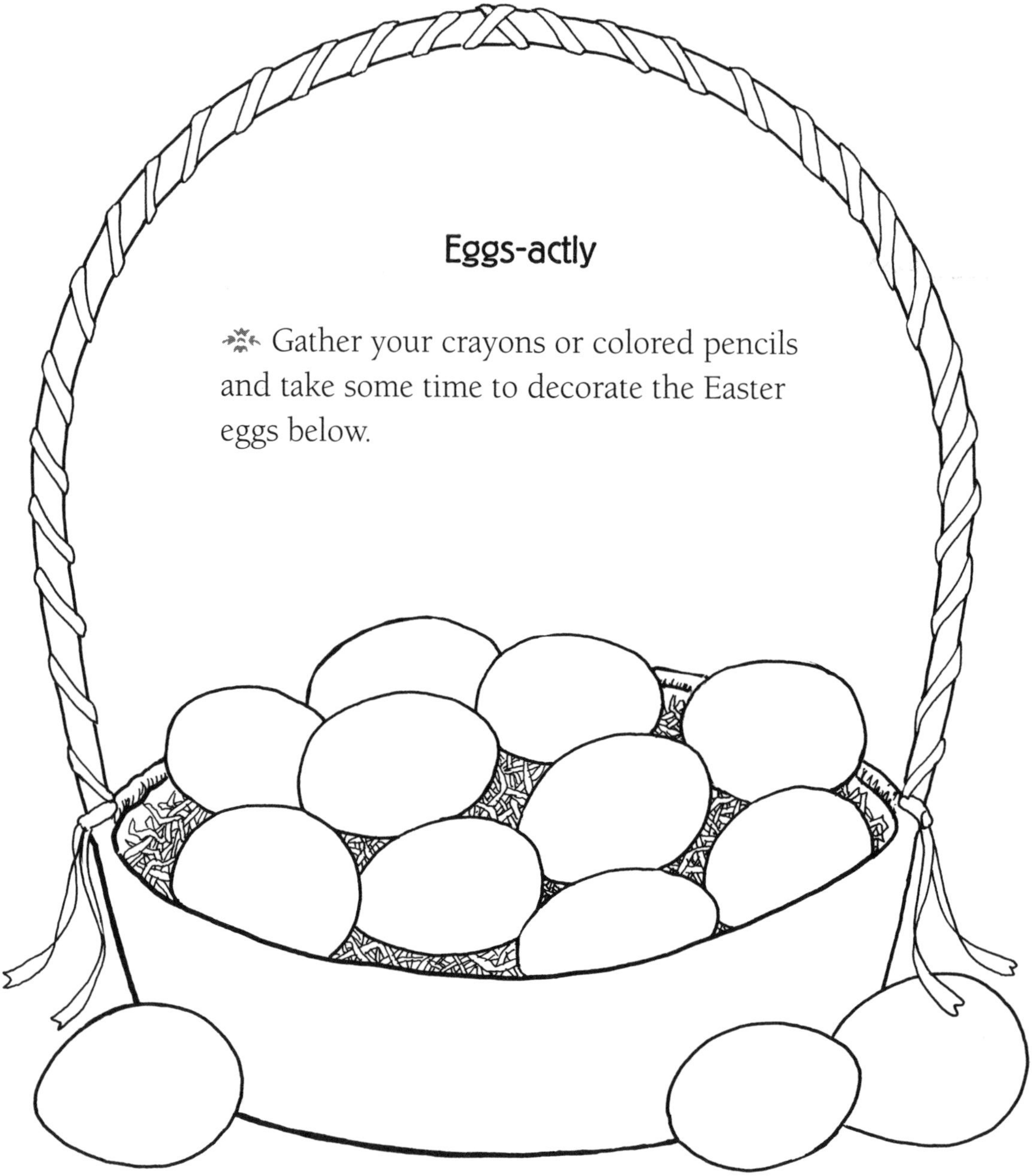

God wants to share eternal life with all of us, including your loved one too.

Light a Candle

On Easter Sunday, or the next time you are in church, you could light a candle in memory of your loved one. An adult will have to do it with you. Most churches ask that you make a small offering when you light a candle. (An offering is a gift of money you give to help others in need.) There's usually a box near the candles where you can put your offering.

Now you're ready to light your candle. While you do it, take a couple of minutes to think about your loved one and to say a prayer.

Once your candle is lit, it will stay lit until it burns out on its own. When that happens, the old candle will be replaced with a new one so that someone else can light it for their special intention. In some churches, the candles are electric—you just press a button and the light bulb lights up. These candles will stayed turned on for about the same amount of time that a regular candle would be lit.

The paschal (PASS-cal) candle is lit during the Easter Season, at baptisms, and at funerals. It stands for the light of Christ risen from the dead. A new candle is used every year, and the year is put onto it. Write the year your loved one died on the paschal candle above to help you remember that Jesus is always with us.

Memorial Day
and Remembrance Day

In the United States, Memorial Day is observed on the last Monday of the month of May. In Canada, Remembrance Day is observed on November 11 (which in the United States is also known as Veterans Day). On these days, we especially remember men and women in the military who have died protecting their countries. We also honor those who continue to serve.

Men and women serve in the military in both peacetime and wartime. Service members who have given their lives to keep us and others safe are heroes. Communities may also pay tribute on these days to firefighters and police officers who have died in the line of duty.

If your loved one served in the military, Memorial Day or Remembrance Day will be even more meaningful for you. Many cities and towns have parades and memorial ceremonies to honor the military as well as others who have served the public. Flags are often flown at half-staff from dawn until noontime. In some communities, small flags are placed at the gravestones of veterans, and families may leave flowers there.

🌺 In the space below, draw a picture of a flag you might see during the memorial events.

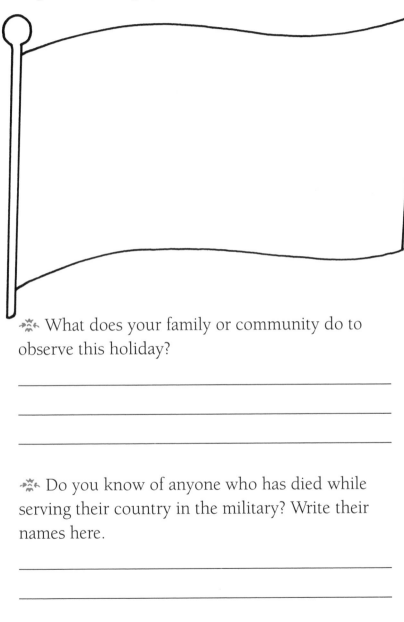

🌺 What does your family or community do to observe this holiday?

_____

_____

_____

🌺 Do you know of anyone who has died while serving their country in the military? Write their names here.

_____

_____

_____

❊ Do you know anyone serving in the military now? Write their names here.

_____

_____

_____

❊ Now say a prayer for peace.

The lines below are part of a prayer that comes from Saint Francis of Assisi. This gentle saint worked and prayed all his life for peace.

Peace Prayer

Lord, make me an instrument
of your peace;
Where there is hatred,
let me sow love.

This simple prayer is asking God to help us to be peaceful people and to spread love wherever we go. What are some things you could do to be a more peaceful person? How could you spread love to others?

Spreading Love

✦ Draw a smiley face or make a check mark next to the things you can do to spread love. Put an X beside the things that wouldn't be so good!

○ Say kind things   ○ Steal

○ Help a friend   ○ Do acts of kindness

○ Try not to argue with others   ○ Share

○ Say mean things   ○ Hit others

○ Yell at someone   ○ Pray

○ Include others in games   ○ Be a good example

○ Leave people out   ○ Be a bully

○ Treat people nicely

✦ Write your other ideas on the lines below.

_____

_____

_____

Feast of All Souls

On November 2, we celebrate the feast of All Souls, sometimes called All Souls' Day. This is a special day when we remember and pray for all those who have died. On All Souls' Day, many people will go to Mass or visit the graves of their loved ones. At the special All Souls' Day Mass, some parishes will make a list of deceased members of the parish. They may place this list on the altar as a special way of remembering these people.

We ask God to take care of everyone who has died and to bring them to be with him in heaven. After a person dies, if they are not quite ready to be in heaven with God, they go through purgatory. Just as we need to prepare and get ready to go to a special party, people need to be ready to go to heaven and celebrate with God.

The souls in purgatory are called "holy souls," and they are happy because they know that soon they will be in heaven. We can pray for everyone in purgatory, and we believe that they—and all the saints in heaven—pray for us, too!

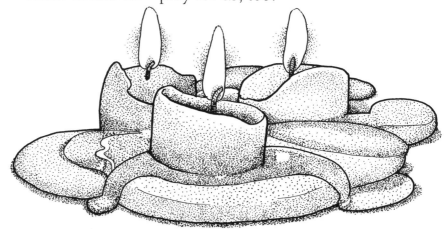

This is a special prayer that is said for the souls of those who have died (it appears on page 37 as well). You can add you loved one's name on the line below:

Prayer for the Dead

Eternal rest grant to them, O Lord, and let perpetual light shine upon them.

May

_____

and the souls of all the faithful departed, through the mercy of God, rest in peace. Amen.

Thanksgiving Day

Thanksgiving is celebrated in Canada on the second Monday in October. In the United States, it's observed on the fourth Thursday in November. No matter where you live, it's a day to gather together with family to celebrate the many blessings God has given us.

It might seem strange this Thanksgiving to think about being thankful. Your loved one has died, so how can someone be thankful after that's happened? But, actually, Thanksgiving is a perfect time to remember your loved one and to give thanks for having had them as part of your life. And it's a perfect time to be thankful that God wants us all to be happy with him in heaven forever.

✻ Put a check mark next to the things that are part of Thanksgiving in your family:

❏ Church   ❏ Saying grace

❏ Turkey   ❏ Board games

❏ Football games   ❏ Pies

❏ Pumpkins   ❏ Candles

❏ Mashed potatoes   ❏ Yams

                       ❏ Autumn leaves

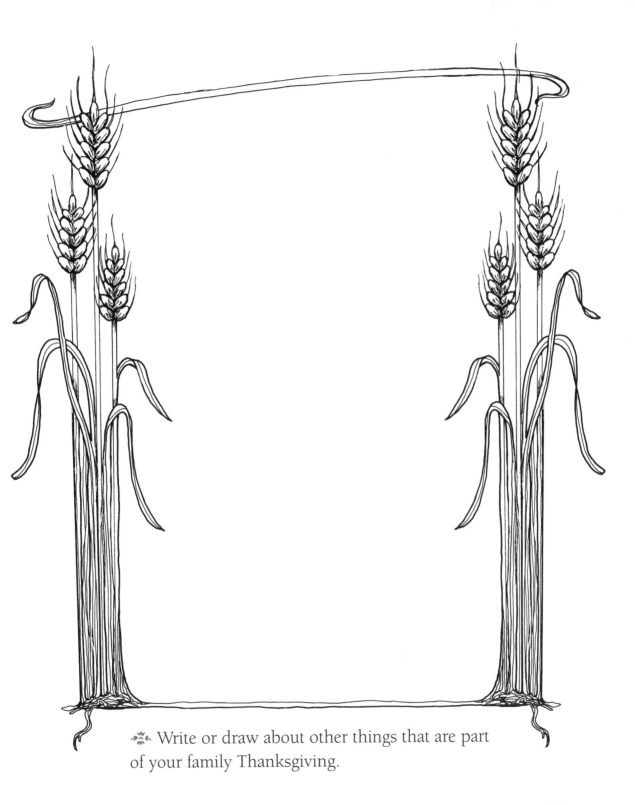

�֍ Write or draw about other things that are part of your family Thanksgiving.

✳ What things about this Thanksgiving will be like last year's?

_____

_____

_____

_____

✳ What things about this Thanksgiving will be different?

_____

_____

_____

_____

✳ If you could change one thing about Thanksgiving, what would it be?

_____

_____

_____

_____

Write your own Thanksgiving Day prayer. It can just be about Thanksgiving Day, or you can make it a special prayer to remember your loved one. Before you begin to write it, think about how you could thank God for your blessings. You can use the ideas below or write your own prayer.

Dear God,

It's Thanksgiving Day, and I thank you for

_____

_____

_____

You've been with me during happy and sad times, and

especially when _____

_____

_____

Today I ask you _____

_____

_____

I know that _____

_____

_____

Amen.

Christmas

Christmas is about celebrating the birth of Jesus. It's also a season when we let others know we're thinking of them by sending cards or giving gifts. People, songs, movies, and ads often tell us that Christmas is the most wonderful time of the year. But after a loved one dies, Christmas might not feel so wonderful, at least not for a while.

Many families have holiday traditions, certain things that they do every year. After a death, some families may feel too sad to follow all their usual traditions. Other families find that following their traditions is a nice way to remember their loved one. However your family decides to handle this situation is fine.

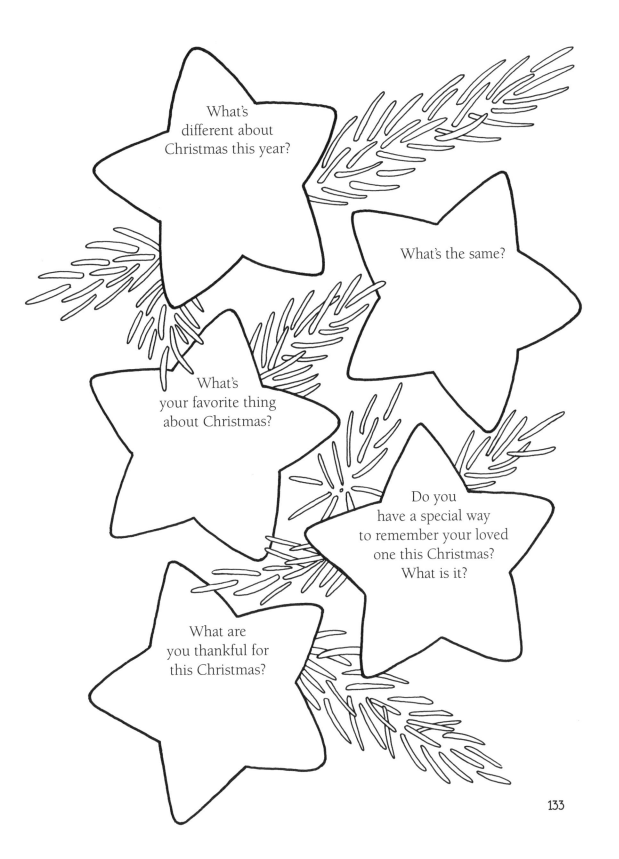

What's different about Christmas this year?

What's the same?

What's your favorite thing about Christmas?

Do you have a special way to remember your loved one this Christmas? What is it?

What are you thankful for this Christmas?

Folded Star Ornament

This is a six-pointed star, also known as a Star of David. It reminds us that Jesus was a descendant of King David.

When you have finished making this ornament, you can write your loved one's name on the front of the star in colored marker, glitter glue, or metallic ink. You can glue or tape a photo of your loved one to the star. You can also make stars for yourself and for other members of your family!

For this activity, you'll need a square piece of paper 6 inches or larger, a pair of scissors, and an ornament hanger or paper clip.

You may want to practice first by using plain white paper. After you've practiced, try making a star out of colored or shiny paper. Tip: A piece of computer paper measures 8-1/2" x 11", so you can cut 2-1/2" off the long side to make an 8-1/2" x 8-1/2" square for your practice star.

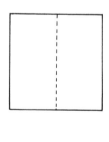

1
Fold your paper in half.

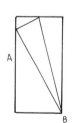

2
Fold the top layer upper right corner so it touches the crease along the side (A). Be sure this fold runs exactly down to the bottom right corner of the paper (B).

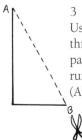

3
Using scissors, cut through both layers of paper along the edge running from point (A) to point (B).

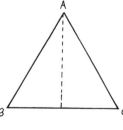

4
Open your paper. Save the triangle (it's exactly the same length on each side). You can discard the other piece of paper.

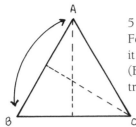

5
Fold point (A) so it touches point (B). Open the triangle up again.

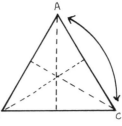

6
Fold point (A) so it touches point (C). Open the triangle up again.

7
Fold point (B) so it touches point (C). Open the triangle up again. The place where all these folds meet should be the exact center of your triangle.

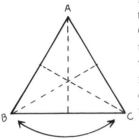

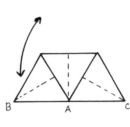

8
Now fold point (A) across so it touches the opposite edge of the triangle. Then fold point (A) back so the new crease touches the exact center of your triangle.

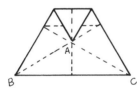

9
Following step 8, do the same folds for point (B), then point (C).

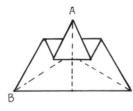

10
Tuck the left-hand corner of pleat (A) under pleat (B), the left-hand corner of pleat (B) under pleat (C), and the left-hand corner of pleat (C) under pleat (A.) This will lock the pleats into place.

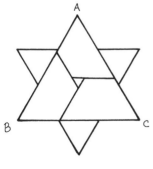

11
Make a small hole at the top of one of the points. Use an ornament hanger or a bent paper clip to hang the star on your Christmas tree.

My One Year Page

The time to look at this page is about one year after your loved one died.

Today's date is _____.

One year ago, this is what I was doing:

_____

Things are different now because:

_____

_____

Here's one enjoyable thing I've done (or would like to do) today: _____

_____

Here's something my family is doing today:

_____

_____

_____

Use your imagination here: If today was a color, what color would it be? _____

Why is that a good color for today?

_____

_____

_____

Here are two questions I have:

_____

_____

If you'd like, share your questions with an adult you trust. Maybe they can help you answer them.

Do you have a special one-year message for the person this book is dedicated to? Write your message here:

_____

_____

_____

Memories

Open your memory box and take out the folded pieces of paper you added from the Acts of Kindness activity on pages 62–63. Read them and remember some of the nice things your loved one did for you or for others.

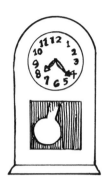

Now That a Year Has Passed . . .

Dear Reader,

A whole year has passed since your loved one died. In some ways, you may be feeling better. In other ways, maybe you're not. It may take longer before you really start to feel better all the time. That's normal and okay.

You've worked hard to read and complete this book as you've been grieving. During this next year,

you may want to reread parts of the book to see how your feelings are continuing to change. You may even want to redo a few pages on a separate piece of paper to see how you feel now that more time has passed. There may be pages that you skipped because they were too painful to complete during the past year. You can finish them this year, or in your own time. If you'd like, you can share this book with trusted adults. Keep the book in a special place, maybe with your memory box or on a bookshelf.

You may still hurt—sometimes a lot. Grief doesn't just go away, not even because a year has gone by. And special events and holidays may sometimes make you feel sadder. It's normal for these feelings of grief to return at different times in our lives. Eventually your heart will heal. And your loved one will always have a special place in your heart—nothing can change that.

Remember all the people here on earth who love and care for you. Talk to them and let them help you. And remember that your loved one and God are always with you. Talk and pray to them, too.

God blesses us always.

Your friend,

Kim

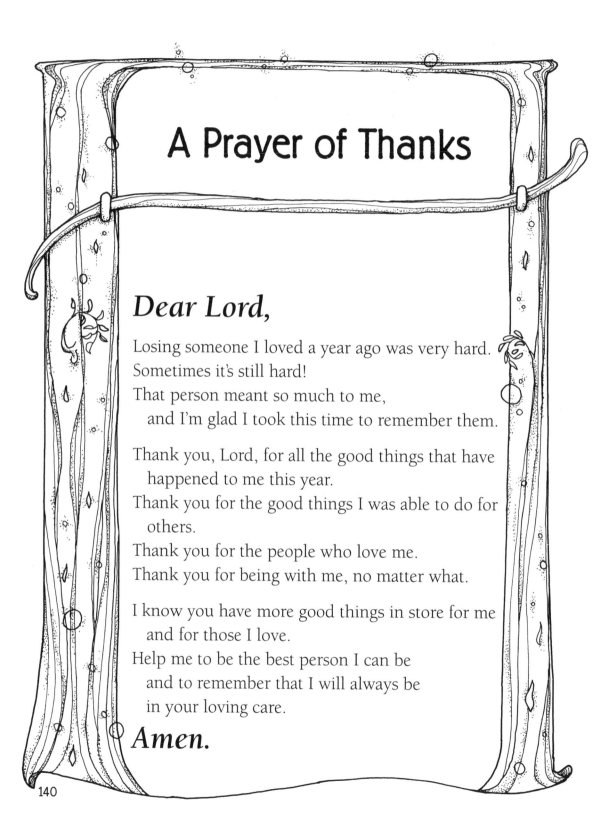

A Prayer of Thanks

Dear Lord,

Losing someone I loved a year ago was very hard.
Sometimes it's still hard!
That person meant so much to me,
and I'm glad I took this time to remember them.

Thank you, Lord, for all the good things that have
happened to me this year.
Thank you for the good things I was able to do for
others.
Thank you for the people who love me.
Thank you for being with me, no matter what.

I know you have more good things in store for me
and for those I love.
Help me to be the best person I can be
and to remember that I will always be
in your loving care.

Amen.

Resources

There are a variety of books available for parents and children on specific grief and loss issues. Search your local library, bookstore, or online book sites to find them. Some suggestions are listed below. Age ranges on the children's books are a general guide. Use your best judgment for books that will be appropriate for your child.

Books for Children

Brown, Laurie Krasny, and Marc Brown. *When Dinosaurs Die: A Guide to Understanding Death*. New York: Little Brown Company Books for Young Readers, 1996.

Through dinosaur characters, this book explores what it means to be alive and dead; feelings, funerals, and customs; saying goodbye; what happens after death; and ways to remember the loved one. Important note: the book covers a variety of ways in which a person may die (old age, illness, accident, war, by an act of another, suicide), but this is handled in an age-appropriate manner. Ages 4–8.

Buscaglia, Leo F. *Fall of Freddie the Leaf: A Story of Life for All Ages*. Thorofare, NJ: SLACK, 1982.

This book explains life and death through the eyes of a leaf named Freddie. Ages 4–8.

Durant, Alan, and Debi Gliori. *Always and Forever*. Orlando: Houghton Mifflin Harcourt, 2004.

Mole, Hare, and Otter try to cope with the loss of their good friend Fox. With the help of Squirrel, they begin to share stories and see that life can go on, even though they still miss Fox. Ages 4–8.

Moser, Adolph, Nancy R. Thatch, and David Melton. *Don't Despair on Thursdays! The Children's Grief Management Book*. Kansas City, KS: Landmark Editions, 1996.

Grief topics included in this book are death, loss, divorce, and moving. The book works to normalize feelings and gives suggestions on how to cope. Ages 9–12.

Mundy, Michaelene, and R. W. Alley. *Sad Isn't Bad: A Good Grief Guide-book for Kids Dealing with Loss.* St. Meinrad, IN: Abbey Press, 1988.

Written with younger children in mind, this book helps to address topics including grief, feelings, and coping with loss. Ages 4–8.

Romain, Trevor. *What on Earth Do You Do When Someone Dies?* Minneapolis: Free Spirit Publishing, 1999.

A question-and-answer book for children that covers various topics related to death, including feelings, funerals, what happens after someone dies, and ways to remember the deceased. Ages 9–12.

Shriver, Maria, and Sandra Speidel. *What's Heaven?* New York: St. Martin's Press, 2007.

While trying to understand the death of her great-grandmother, a young girl's questions about death, funerals, heaven, and our souls are explained. Ages 4–8.

Thomas, Pat, and Lesley Harker. *I Miss You: A First Look at Death.* Hauppauge, NY: Barron's Educational Series, 2000.

The book explains death, discusses feelings and coping, and asks some questions of the reader regarding their personal experiences and feelings. Ages 4–8.

Books for Adults

Curley, Terence P. *Healing: Questions and Answers for Those Who Mourn.* New York: Alba House, 2001.

Written in a question-and-answer format, this book looks at healing through the lens of faith and spirituality. It examines the phases of loss and transition through Catholic understanding, teachings, and prayer.

Kroen, William C., and Pamela Espeland. *Helping Children Cope with the Loss of a Loved One.* Minneapolis: Free Spirit Publishing, 1996.

This title explores children's grief from infancy though age eighteen, ways children at different ages cope and react to loss, how to guide and support the child through grief, and gives suggestions on remembering and moving on.

Poust, Mary DeTurris. *Parenting a Grieving Child: Helping Children Find Faith, Hope, and Healing after the Loss of a Loved One.* Chicago: Loyola Press, 2002.

This book looks at grief and loss while weaving faith throughout. Topics include explaining death and traumatic loss, supporting the child both emotionally and spiritually, and helping them to adjust, remember, and move on. Each chapter contains tips and activities to guide the reader in more specific and concrete ways.

Schaefer, Dan, and Christine Lyons. *How Do We Tell the Children?* New York: Newmarket Press, 2001.

The book examines what children from ages two to teen think of death, ways to tell children about death and dying based on the type of loss, grieving and healing at different ages, and saying good-bye.

Online Resources

The American Academy of Child and Adolescent Psychiatry. "Children and Grief." *Facts for Families* No. 8 (2008). http://www.aacap.org/cs/root/facts_for_families/children_and_grief

Facts and tips regarding children and grief are discussed.

Goodman, Robin F. "Children and Grief: What They Know, How They Feel, How to Help." NYU Child Study Center. http://www.about-ourkids.org/articles/children_grief_what_they_know_how_they_feel_how_help

This article discusses grief and how to help (infants through adolescents).

Center for Loss and Life Transition: www.Centerforloss.com

Directed by speaker and author Alan Wolfelt, PhD, this Colorado Center also offers online resources for kids who grieve, their friends and family members, as well as grief counselors.

Children's Grief Education Association: http://www.childgrief.org

The site offers a variety of information, including pages with activities for children and teens. Use the "Children & Grief" tab to link to information for parents and teachers, children's grief responses, and "Ways to Help" chart, as well as other helpful links and pages (for example, newsletter information, military family information, and suicide).

GriefNet.org: http://www.GriefNet.org

Find and join support groups for adults and children, create memorials, and locate resources (books and Web sites). This site also links to specific memorials (for example, Hurricane Katrina).

KIDSAID.com: http://kidsaid.com

This site is connected to GriefNet.org and is designed specifically for children. The site gives children the opportunity to ask questions and share stories and artwork. Use the "young child" link for information on children and the grieving process.

More Resources

Some states have specific organizations that offer support and other services. Search online for specific groups in your area. You can also explore local funeral homes and hospitals for support groups and other support programs.

BOOKS & MEDIA

The Daughters of St. Paul operate book and media centers at the following addresses. Visit, call or write the one nearest you today, or find us on the World Wide Web, www.pauline.org

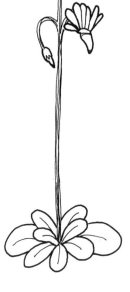

CALIFORNIA

3908 Sepulveda Blvd
Culver City, CA 90230
310-397-8676

935 Brewster Avenue
Redwood City, CA 94063
650-369-4230

5945 Balboa Avenue
San Diego, CA 92111
858-565-9181

FLORIDA

145 S.W. 107th Avenue
Miami, FL 33174
305-559-6715

HAWAII

1143 Bishop Street
Honolulu, HI 96813
808-521-2731
Neighbor Islands call:
866-521-2731

ILLINOIS

172 North Michigan Avenue
Chicago, IL 60601
312-346-4228

LOUISIANA

4403 Veterans Memorial Blvd
Metairie, LA 70006
504-887-7631

MASSACHUSETTS

885 Providence Hwy
Dedham, MA 02026
781-326-5385

MISSOURI

9804 Watson Road
St. Louis, MO 63126
314-965-3512

NEW YORK

64 West 38th Street
New York, NY 10018
212-754-1110

PENNSYLVANIA

Relocating
215-676-9494

SOUTH CAROLINA

243 King Street
Charleston, SC 29401
843-577-0175

VIRGINIA

1025 King Street
Alexandria, VA 22314
703-549-3806

CANADA

3022 Dufferin Street
Toronto, ON M6B 3T5
416-781-9131